A STRAIGHTFORWARD GUIDE

TO

CONTRACT LAW

Peter Clarke

Editor: Roger Sproston

Straightforward Guides
www.straightforwardco.co.uk

Straightforward Guides

British Cataloguing in Publication data. A catalogue record is available for this book from the British Library.

ISBN

978-1-913776-03-9

Printed in the United Kingdom by 4edge www.4edge.co.uk

Cover Design by BW Studios

Contents

Table of cases

**

Table of Cases (Alphabetical Order)

****

Ch. 1

Introduction to Contract Law

A Straightforward Guide to Contract law updated to January **2021** is a comprehensive and easy to understand introduction to the complex area of contract law.

The book covers key changes to contract law that arise from the introduction of the Consumer Rights Act 2015 and also key considerations which have arisen following the onset of COVID 19. The full fallout, and the effect on contract law, of the exit of the UK from the European Union (BREXIT) on December 31st 2020 has yet to be felt.

COVID 19 and the effects on contract law

Currently, of more immediate importance, are the effects on contract law following the onset of COVID 19, which mainly concern consumer contracts, for example contracts with travel companies, and also frustration of contract and *force majeure*. We discuss force majeure and frustration of contract in chapter nine and also the effect on consumer contracts in Chapter ten.

Many people, either knowingly or unknowingly, enter into contracts without fully understanding the implications of what they are doing. Contracts can cover a number of areas, from hire purchase agreements to more complex finance agreements, contracts for construction of buildings, contracts for work around the house or contracts to supply goods. Notwithstanding the type of contract or what area of life it relates to, there is a comprehensive framework of law, both in statute and also common law, which covers parties to a contract. This book will enable the reader, whether layperson or professional, to obtain the basic facts about contract law and also to see clearly where they stand in relation to their rights and obligations. Throughout the book there is reference to relevant court cases.

The necessity of contract law

Contract law is necessary because the law only enforces certain types of promises, basically those promises that involve some sort of exchange. A promise for which nothing is given in return is called a gratuitous promise, and is not usually enforceable in law (the exception being where the promise is put into some sort of document, usually a deed).

The main reason that we need contract law is because of the complex society we live in, a capitalist society. In capitalist society people trade freely on many different levels. There are many complex interactions, from small business endeavors to massive projects, such as construction projects where binding agreements are essential. Contract law is there to provide a framework to regulate activities. Contract law will rarely force an individual or company to fulfill contractual promises. What it does do is to try to compensate innocent parties financially, usually by attempting to put them in a position that they would have been in if the contract had been performed as agreed.

Contract law-a brief history

Contract law, or the origins of contract law, goes back more than three hundred years. However, because of the very fast innovations in technology and the industrial revolution generally, the main body of contract law was established in the nineteenth century. Before that, contract law barely existed as a separate area of law. Before the nineteenth century there were many areas of life where free negotiation was not an issue. Activities such as buying goods and then selling them on in the same market were illegal and were criminal offences. There was a basic right to a reasonable standard of living and no one was expected to negotiate that standard for their selves. A similar, though less humane approach was taken to relationships between employer and employee, or master and servant as they were then called.

Today, we all expect to have an employment contract detailing hours of work, duties and pay. This is the most basic of perceived rights.

We may, in most cases, not be able to negotiate the terms, but at least it is a contract. In a status society (as it was called), employment obligations were quite simply derived from whether you were a master or a servant: masters were entitled to ask servants to do more or less anything, and an employee who refused would or could face criminal sanctions. Employers had less onerous obligations that could sometimes include supplying food or medical

17

care. Both sets of obligations were seen as fixed and non-negotiable.

Along with the development of contract law within a rapidly changing laissez faire society, came a rapidly changing political consciousness. The view arose that society was no more than a collection of self-interested individuals, each of whom was the best judge of their own interests, and should as far as possible be left alone to pursue those interests. This laissez faire approach gave birth to the law of contract, as we know it, in that, as we have seen, where people make their own transactions, unregulated by the state, it is important that they keep their promises.

Freedom of contract

Its origins in the laissez faire doctrine of the nineteen-century have had enormous influence on the development of contract law. The most striking reflection of this is the importance traditionally placed on freedom of contract. This doctrine promotes the idea that since parties are the best judges of their own interests, they should be free to make contracts on any terms they choose-on the most basic assumption that no one would choose unfavorable terms. The courts role is to act as umpire holding the parties to their promises, not to ask whether the bargain made was a fair one. However, there are many problems with the freedom of contract:

- Inequality of bargaining strength between the two parties
- The acceptance of implied terms
- The use of standard form contracts

- Statutory intervention to protect consumers; and
- The obligation to implement EU law.

Over the years, courts have moved away from their reluctance to intervene, sometimes through their own making sometimes through parliament, notably the Unfair Contract Terms Act 1997.

Contracts and the notion of fairness

Traditional contract law lays down rules that are designed to apply in any contractual situation, regardless who the parties are, their relationships to each other and the subject matter of a contract. The basis for this approach is derived from the *laissez-faire* belief that parties should be left alone to make their own bargains. It was thought that the law should be required simply to provide a framework, allowing parties to know what they had to do to make their agreements binding.

This framework was intended to treat everyone equally, since to make different rules for one type of contracting party than for another would be to intervene in the fairness of the bargain. As a result the same rules were applied to contracts in which both parties had equal bargaining power as to those where one party had significantly less economic power, or legal or technical knowledge, such as a consumer contract.

This approach, often called procedural fairness, or formal justice, was judged to be fair because it treats everyone equally, favoring no one. There are, however, big problems inherent in this approach in that, if people are unequal to begin with, treating them equally simply maintains the inequality.

Over the last century the law has, to some extent at least, moved away from procedural fairness, and an element of substantive fairness, or distributive justice has developed. Substantive fairness aims to redress the imbalance of power between parties, giving some protection to the weaker one. For example, terms are now implied into employment contracts so that employers cannot simply dismiss employees without reasonable grounds for doing so. Similar protections have been given to others, such as tenants and consumers.

The objective approach
Contract law claims to be about enforcing obligations that the parties have voluntarily assumed. Bearing in mind that contracts do not have to be in writing, it is clear that enforcing contract law might be a problem. Even where contracts are in writing important areas may be left out. Contract law's approach to this problem is to look for the appearance of consent. This approach was explained by Blackburn J in Smith v Hughes (1871)-

" if, whatever a man's real intentions may be, he so conducts himself that a reasonable man would believe he was assenting to the terms proposed by the other party and that other party upon that belief enters into the contract with him, the man thus conducting himself would be equally bound as if he had intended to agree to the other party's terms".

It can be seen that the area of contract law is complex and yet is governed by basic principles. In this book we cover, amongst other areas:

- Contracts and the law generally
- The formation of a contract
- The terms of a contract
- Implied terms
- Misrepresentation
- Remedies if a contract is breached.

A basic understanding of contracts will prove invaluable to any person who takes the time to understand more. This brief book will enable the reader to obtain that basic understanding.

Finally, keep an eye on BREXIT, and the ramification of this, mainly the interaction between Britain and the EU in terms of law.

****

Ch. 2

Forming a Contract

In this chapter we look at the main principles underpinning forming a contract. We look at the nature of contracts and the notion of offer and acceptance plus certainty of contract and terms implied into a contract. The intention to create legal relations is examined along with different types of contract and capacity to enter into a contract. We also look into electronic contracts and signatures plus contracts for software.

Underpinning all contracts are four main principles:

1) A contract is an agreement between the parties to that contract-one person makes an offer and the other accepts that offer

2) Both parties have an intention to be legally bound by the agreement-this is usually known as an intention to create legal relations

3) Parties to the agreement need to be absolutely clear as to the terms of the agreement – this is the main area of contention with contracts, as we will see later

4) There must be consideration provided by each of the parties to the contract – this means that one person promises to give or deliver and the other promises to pay. The offer and the payment – either monetary or in kind - is the consideration.

When making a contract, or entering into a contract all parties to the contract must have the legal capacity to enter into a contract. Very importantly, a contract, in most cases, does not have to be in writing – a piece of paper is not necessary, the agreement and evidence of that agreement forms the basis of contract. There are a few important exceptions, including contracts relating to interests in land (Law of property (Miscellaneous Provisions) Act 1989, s 2(1) and consumer credit (Consumer Credit Act 1974). We will outline those contracts that do need to be in writing later on in this chapter. Other factors affecting formation include:

- Form-the way the contract is created (e.g. the sale of land can only be made in the form of a deed). Form is an issue with specialty contracts but not with simple contracts
- Privity of contract and the rights of third parties-generally a contract is only enforceable by or against a party to it, subject to exceptions and certain third party rights are now protected in the Contracts (Rights of Third Parties) Act 1999.

The nature of contracts – unilateral and bilateral contracts
The majority of contracts entered into are known as bilateral contracts. This quite simply means that each party to a contract agrees to take on an obligation. This obligation is underpinned by a promise to give something to the other party. A unilateral contract will arise where one party to the contract will make a promise to do something (usually to pay a sum of money) if the other party carries out a certain task. Examples of this are where you might undertake

to pay someone a sum of money if they shave off their hair for charity or give up smoking. Estate agents enter into unilateral contracts whereby a percentage of sales go to the agent if they sell the property. However, the agent is not legally bound to sell the property, just to try to sell it.

The notion of offer and acceptance

As we have seen, for a contract to have legal status, usually one of the parties to the contract must have made an offer and the other party must have accepted the offer. Once the contract is accepted the agreement will be legally binding. The person making the offer is called the offeror and the person to whom the offer is made is known as the offeree. An offer may be express or implied. Express means that there is an express intention to offer goods and for X to pay an amount for the goods. Implied may mean, for example, when purchasing something from a store. The act of taking goods to a checkout means that there is an implied offer to buy those goods.

When dealing with contracts, or the formation of a contract most offers are made to specific parties. However, offers can also be made to a group of people or to the public at large. One such example is where a reward is offered for information following a crime. One famous case dealing with offers to the public at large is Carlill v Carbolic Smokeball (1893) the defendants in this case were the manufacturers of 'smokeballs' popular at the time, which they claimed could prevent flu. They published adverts to this effect stating that anyone using their smoke balls and not being cured of flu would receive £100.

One person buying their smokeballs was a Mrs Carlill. It did not work and she claimed the £100. The manufacturers argument was to claim that their advert did not constitute a contract, since it was impossible to contract with the whole wide world. They claimed that they were not legally bound to pay the money. The court, needless to say, rejected this argument, which held that the advert did contract with the world. Mrs Carlill accepted the offer and duly claimed the £100. A contract such as the one above is usually a unilateral contract.

The invitation to treat
Certain kinds of transactions between parties might involve a preliminary stage where one party to the contract invites the other party to make an offer. This preliminary stage is known as 'invitation to treat'.

One such case that demonstrates this is that of Gibson v Manchester City Council (1979). In this case, a council tenant of Manchester City Council expressed an interest in buying their house. The application was duly completed and sent to the council. A letter was received from the council stating that it may be prepared to sell the house to the tenant for £2180. The tenant, Mr. Gibson, queried the purchase price pointing out that the path to the house was in bad condition. The council refused to alter the price, stating that the valuation reflected the condition of the property and the current property market. Mr Gibson then wrote asking the council to continue with the sale. Following a change in the control of the council, and a new political approach, it was decided to stop the sale of houses to tenants. Mr Gibson was informed that his application had been declined, notwithstanding the initial offer. Legal proceedings were brought against the council claiming that the letter received by Mr Gibson, with the offer of sale at a price, constituted a contract, and was an offer which he duly accepted. The House of Lords, however, ruled that the council had not made an offer, the letter stating the purchase price was merely one step in the negotiations for a contract and amounted only to an invitation to treat. Its purpose in the first instance was quite simply to invite the making of a formal application, amounting to an offer, from the tenant.

Retailers websites

These are probably invitations to treat, although this has no clear definition at the moment. Regulation 12 of the E-Commerce (EC Directives) Regulations 2002 suggests that the customers order may well be the offer so that the website is an invitation to treat.

Offers of sale in shops

Goods in shop windows marked with a price are generally regarded as invitations to treat, rather than offers to actually sell the goods at the price displayed. One such case highlighting this is *Fisher v Bell (1961)* where a shopkeeper was prosecuted under the Offensive Weapons Act 1959 for 'offering for sale' an offensive weapon. The shopkeeper was displaying a flick knife with a price attached in the window. It was held that the display of the flick knife was an invitation to treat, rather than an offer, thus the shopkeeper was

27

found not guilty of the offence. Where goods are sold on a self-service basis, the customer will make an offer to purchase on presenting the goods at the till and the shopkeeper may reject or accept that offer. One case which highlights this is *Pharmaceutical Society of Great Britain v Boots Cash Chemists (Southern) Limited 1953*. Boots were charged with an offence concerning the sale of items, medicines that could only be sold under the supervision of a qualified pharmacist. Two customers in a self-service shop selected the items, which were marked with a price from a shelf in the shop. The shelves were not supervised by a pharmacist but the pharmacist was instructed to supervise at the cash desk. The issue was whether the sale had taken place at the shelf or the cash desk.

The Court of Appeal decided that the shelf display was like an advertisement and was therefore an invitation to treat. The offer was made by the customer when the items were placed in a basket and was only accepted when the goods were taken to the cash desk. A pharmacist was supervising at that point so no offence was committed. Following on from this principle, shops do not have to sell goods at the marked price and a customer cannot insist on buying a particular good on display. Displaying the goods is not an offer so a customer cannot accept it making a binding contract. (In reality, if shops do display goods at a price they generally sell it at that price although, as we have seen they do not have to).

Contracts and advertisements
A distinction is generally made between advertisements for unilateral contracts and advertisements for bilateral contracts.

28

Advertisements for unilateral contracts will include those such as described in the case of Carlill and Carbolic Smokeball Co or those offering a reward for information or for lost property. They are usually treated as offers on the basis that no further negotiations are needed between the parties to the offer and the person making the offer will usually be bound by it.

One case is that of *Bowerman v Association of British Travel Agents Ltd (1996)* in which a school had booked a skiing holiday with a travel agent, which was a member of ABTA. Any member of ABTA has to display a notice as follows:

Where holidays or other travel arrangements have not yet commenced at the time of failure of the tour operator, ABTA arranges for you to be reimbursed the money you have paid for your holiday.

In this case the tour operator became insolvent and all holidays were cancelled. The school was refunded the money paid for the holiday but not the cost of the travel insurance taken out, which was significant. The case was taken to court and ABTA lost because the notice constituted an offer which the school accepted by contracting with the ABTA member.

Bilateral contracts

Bilateral contracts are the types that advertise specified goods at a certain price such as those found in shop windows and in magazines. They are usually considered invitations to treat on the grounds that they may lead to further bargaining. One such case that highlights this is *Partridge v Crittendon (1968)*. An advertisement in a magazine stated 'Bramblefinch cocks and hens 25shillings each'. As the Bramblefinch was a protected species, the person who placed the advert was charged with unlawfully offering for sale a wild bird which was against the Protection of Birds Act 1954, but the conviction was quashed on the grounds that the advertisement was not an offer but an invitation to treat.

Communication of offers

A valid offer must be communicated to the offeree. It would be unfair for a person to be bound by an offer of which he had no knowledge. This is reflected in *Taylor v Laird 1856*. The offeree must have clear knowledge of the existence of an offer for it to be enforceable. This is reflected in *Inland Revenue Commissioners v Fry 2001*.

An offer can be made to one individual or to the whole world, when the offer can be accepted by any party who had genuine notice of it. In addition, the terms of the contract must be certain. The parties must know in advance what they are contracting over, so any vague words may invalidate the agreement. this is reflected in *Guthing v Lynn 1831*.

The length of time an offer should last

An offer may cease to exist in any of the following circumstances:

-Where an offeror states that an offer will be open for a specified time

-Where the offeror has not specified how long the offer will remain open, the offer will lapse after a reasonable length of time has passed. How much time can be deemed reasonable will depend on whether the offer was communicated quickly and also on the subject matter.

Some offers are made subject to certain specified conditions, and if these conditions are not in place, the offer may lapse. An offer may lapse if and when the offeree rejects it. For example, if A offers to sell B a car on Tuesday, and B says no, B cannot come back on Wednesday and insist on accepting the offer

A counter offer can terminate the original offer. One case that highlights this is *Hyde v Wrench (1840)* where the defendant offered to sell his farm for £1000 and the plaintiff responded by offering to buy it at £950-this is termed making a counter offer. The farm owner refused to sell at that price and when the plaintiff later tried to buy the farm at £1000, the original asking price, it was held that this offer was no longer available. The counter offer had terminated the original offer

The death of the offeror can affect the offer. If the offeree knows of the death of the offeror then the offer is terminated. If they did not, the offer still stands, although this is one area of law that is still unclear. It very much depends on the circumstances at the time

An offer may be revoked, withdrawn, at any time until it has been accepted. This is the basic rule, although there are a number of other principles. It is not enough for an offeror simply to change his or her mind about an offer. The offeror must notify the offeree that the offer has been revoked. Revocation does not specifically have to be communicated by the offeror, it can be by another reliable party.

Acceptance of an offer

For acceptance to be valid the following conditions must be met:

- Acceptance must be communicated to the seller: the buyer must receive the acceptance to be effective (*Entorres v Miles Far East* (1955)); silence will not suffice (*Felthouse v Bindley* (1862)); acceptance can be made through conduct (*Butler Machine Tool v Ex-cell-o Corporation* (1979)).
- The terms of the acceptance must exactly match the terms of the offer: if the terms are not the same, this will actually be a counter offer and no contract will have arisen (*Hyde v Wrench* (1840)).
- The agreement must be certain (see below).

Consideration is something of legal value which is given in exchange for something else. It can be anything of value (eg, money, property, or a service), which each party to a legally binding contract must agree to exchange if the contract is to be valid. In *Currie v Misa* (1875), Lush J referred to consideration as consisting of a detriment to the promisee or a benefit to the promisor. He described it as: '...some right, interest, profit or benefit accruing to one party, or some forebearance, detriment, loss or responsibility given, suffered or undertaken by the other.'

Certainty of agreement

Even though the parties may have appeared to make an agreement by the exchange of a matching offer and acceptance, the courts may refuse to enforce it if there appears to be uncertainty about what has been agreed, or if some important aspect of the agreement is left open to be decided later.

In *Scammell v Ouston* (1941), for example, the parties had agreed to the supply of a lorry on 'hire purchase terms'. The House of Lords held that in the absence of any other evidence of the details of the hire purchase agreement this was too vague to be enforceable, and there was therefore no contract.

Acceptance of an offer must be unconditional, accepting the precise terms of the offer. Where the process of negotiation is long and difficult, it might be difficult to pinpoint exactly when an offer has been made and accepted. In such cases a court will examine the precise course of negotiations to ascertain whether the parties have reached agreement, if at all and when. This process can be complicated when the so-called 'battle of forms' occurs. Rather than negotiating terms each time a contract is made many companies try to use standard conditions, which will be printed on headed stationary, such as order forms and delivery notes. The 'battle of forms' occurs when one party sends a form stating that the contract is on their terms, and the other party responds by sending back the forms and stating that the contract is on their terms. The general rule in these cases is that the 'last shot' wins the battle. Each new form issued is treated as a counter offer, so that when one party performs its obligation under the contract the action will be seen as acceptance by the other side. One simple case that illustrates this is British Road Services v Crutchley (Arthur V) Ltd (1968). The plaintiffs delivered some whisky to the defendants for storage. The BRS driver handed the defendants a delivery note, which listed the company's terms of carriage. The note was accepted and stamped with Crutchley's terms and conditions and the court held that by accepting this, the BRS driver had accepted a counter offer. Although many cases are simple, other more recent case law has held that the last shot will not always succeed.

It is a basic assumption that there is no acceptance until the act has been thoroughly performed. However, in some cases, part performance may amount to acceptance. In *Errington v Errington (1952)* a father bought a house in his own name for £750, borrowing £500 of the price from a building society. He bought the house for his son and daughter in law to live in, and told them that they must meet the mortgage repayments. If they met the payments the house would be signed over to them on completion of the term. The couple moved in and began to pay the mortgage, but they never in fact made the promise to continue with the payments until the mortgage was paid off, which meant that the contract was unilateral.

When the father later died, the people in charge of his affairs sought to withdraw the offer. The Court of Appeal held that it was too late to do this. The part performance of the son and daughter in law constituted an acceptance of the contract and the father and his representatives after death were bound by the resulting contract unless the son and daughter in law ceased the payments, in which

34

case the offer was no longer binding. A request for information about an offer does not constitute a counter offer, so the original offer remains open. If an offeree has to accept an offer in a specified manner, then only acceptance by that method or an equally effective one will be binding

Communicating acceptance of an offer

An acceptance will not usually take effect until it is clearly communicated to the offeror. However, there are some circumstances where acceptance may take effect without it being communicated to the offeror. An offer may clearly state, or indeed imply, that acceptance need not be communicated to the offeror. An offeror who fails to receive an acceptance through their own fault may be prevented from claiming that the non-communication means they should not be bound by the contract.

The general rule for acceptances by post is that they take effect when they are posted, rather than when they are communicated. The postal rule was laid down in the case of *Adams v Lindsell (1818)*, when on the 2nd of September 1817, the defendants wrote to the plaintiffs, who were in the wool processing business, offering to sell them a quantity of sheep fleeces, and stating that they required an answer 'in course of post'. However, the defendants did not address the letter correctly and it did not reach the plaintiffs until the evening of September the 5th. The plaintiffs posted their acceptance the same evening, and it reached the defendants on the 9th of September. If the original letter had been correctly addressed it would have reached the plaintiffs by the 7th of September.

Because it was incorrectly addressed it did not and no reply was received and the wool was sold to a third party. The issue was whether a sale had been made before the sale of the wool to the third party. The court heard that the contract was concluded as soon as the acceptance was posted and that the defendants were bound from the evening of 5th September so should not have sold the wool to a third party. There are certain exceptions to the postal rule. The offeror may avoid the postal rule by making it a specific term of their offer that acceptance will only take effect when it is communicated to them.

The postal rule has limited application to modern communications technology. In *Entores Ltd v Miles Far East Corp*, offer and acceptance communicated by telex were valid because the method was so instantaneous that the parties were deemed to be dealing as if face-to-face, even though they were in different countries. The time when these forms of communication are used may cause problems in determining if a contract is made, as when a fax is sent out of office hours. Now offer and acceptance in the case of electronic communication is governed by the Consumer Contracts (Information, Cancellation and Additional Charges) Regulations 2013 which replaced the Consumer Protection (Distance Selling) Regulations 2000. This gives the buyer the right to be informed of the right to cancel within seven days, description, price, arrangements for payment and identity of seller, and to be given written confirmation, without which a contract is not formed. Under EU Electronic Commerce Directive 2000/31 no contract can be made electronically until the buyer has received acknowledgement of his acceptance. the Directive has been implemented through the Electronic Commerce (EC Directive) Regulations 2000.

Ignorance of the offer

It is generally accepted that a person cannot accept an offer of which they are unaware, because in order to create a binding contract, the parties must reach agreement. This is a very important principle.

Tenders, auctions and the sale of land

The rules outlined above also apply to the sale of land and to sales by tender and auction. If a large organization, such as a company or government department needs to contract a supplier of goods or services, it will, more often than not, advertise for tenders, i.e., bids. Organizations wishing to supply goods or services will reply, detailing price for these services. The advertiser will choose from the replies and contact the successful tender. As a general rule, the request for tenders is regarded as an invitation to treat, (see previous) so there is no specific obligation to accept any of the tenders sent. The tenders themselves are offers and a contract does not come into existence until one is accepted. However, where a party has issued an invitation to tender, it is bound to consider all correctly submitted tenders. One such case highlighting this is *Blackpool and Fylde Aero Club v Blackpool Borough Council (1990)*. Blackpool BC invited tenders from people who were interested in operating leisure flights from the local airfield. Tenders had to be submitted to the town hall by a stated deadline. The Aero Club submitted its application on time but the council refused to consider it, as due to an error on their part, they mistakenly believed that the tender had been submitted after the deadline.

It was held that the council's invitation to tender was a unilateral offer to consider all tenders which fell within its rules. The tender constituted an offer which had been accepted by the Aero Club. The offer was accepted by any party who put in a tender. Thus the council were obliged to consider all tenders (acceptances) to their offer, including the Aero Club tender. They were not, of course, obliged to accept the tender. In some cases however, an invitation for tenders may in itself be an offer. The main example of this is where the invitation to tender makes it clear that the lowest tender (or highest) will be accepted. The implications of choosing to accept a tender depend on what sort of tender is involved.

Specific tenders

Where an invitation to tender specifies that a particular quantity of goods is required on a particular date, or between certain dates, agreeing to one of the tenders submitted will constitute acceptance of an offer, creating a contract between the parties.

Non-specific tenders

Some invitations to tender are not specific, and may for example simply state that certain goods may be required, up to a particular maximum quantity, with deliveries to be made if and when requested. For example, an invitation to tender made by a hospital may ask for tenders to supply goods, if and when required. In this case, taking up one of the tenders submitted does not amount to acceptance of an offer in the contractual sense and there is no contract. The hospital may take the goods all at once, some at a time or none at all. It is not bound.

Auction sales

The parties to an auction sale are the bidder and the owner of the goods. The auctioneer supplies a service and is not party to the contract between buyer and seller.

Sale of land

The standard rules of contract apply to the sale of land, including buildings. However, the court applies the rules strictly in the case of land, tending to require very clear evidence of an intention to be bound before they will state that an offer has been made.

In *Harvey v Facey (1893)* the plaintiffs sent the defendants a telegram asking 'will you sell us Bumper Hall Pen? Telegraph lowest cash price'. The reply arrived back stating 'Lowest price for Bumper Hall pen £900'. The plaintiffs then sent a telegram saying 'we agree to buy Bumper Hall Pen for £900. Please send us your title deeds'. On these facts, the Privy Council held that there was no contract. They regarded the telegram from the defendants as a statement of price only. It was therefore not an offer which could be accepted by the third telegram.

In practice there are rigid procedures involved in the sale of land. The first is the 'sale subject to contract', where the parties agree to the sale and the implication is that there is a good deal of proving and other work before a contract is in existence. The next stage is the exchange of contract, where the buyer and seller agree to the terms of the formal contract. Once the contracts are exchanged then the contract is binding and any backing out can result in a claim for damages and lost deposit.

Certainty of contract

In order to be viewed as a binding contract, an agreement must be absolutely certain. That is, it should not be vague or incomplete. One such case that amplifies this is that of *Scammell v Ouston (1941)* where the parties agreed that Ouston could buy a van from Scammell, giving his lorry in part exchange paying the balance over two-years on hire purchase terms. Scammell decided to back out and claimed that there was no contract between the parties. The House of Lords agreed, pointing out that the courts would uphold an agreement if there really was one, in this case the terms were too vague, particularly the agreement to pay on Hire Purchase Terms. In certain cases, parties may leave details vague, particularly when dealing with fluctuating prices and other factors. Provisions should be in the contract stating how they should be clarified.

Terms implied into contract by statute

In some cases, statute will override contract and will provide that certain provisions should be read into contracts even though they have not been specifically agreed between the parties. For example, under the Consumer Rights Act 2015, an agreement for the sale of goods can become binding as soon as the parties have agreed to buy and sell, with the details of the contract being laid down by law, or determined by the standard of reasonableness. In such a case, the parties do not even have had to agree on a price. The buyer is entitled to pay a reasonable price. Terms implied by statute will be examined further on in this book.

Intention to create legal relations

One major principle of contract law is that of intention to create legal relations. If two or more parties make an agreement without the intention of being legally bound by it, the agreement will not be regarded as a contract. As far as intent to be legally bound is concerned, contracts can be divided into domestic and social agreements on one hand, and commercial agreements on the other. Where the agreement falls into the former category there is an assumption that the parties do not intend to create legal relations. The reverse is true when it comes to commercial agreements.

Domestic and social agreements

Where a husband and wife who are living together as one household make an agreement, the courts will assume that they do not intend to be legally bound, unless the agreement states other wise. In *Balfour v Balfour (1919)* the defendant was a civil servant stationed in Sri Lanka. Whilst the couple were on leave in England, Mrs. Balfour was taken ill, and it became clear that her husband would have to return by himself. He promised to pay her maintenance of £30 per month. They eventually separated and the

41

husband refused to make any more payments. The Court of Appeal decided he was not bound to make further payments, as when the agreement was made there was no intention to create legal relations. Likewise, agreements between parents and children are assumed not to be legally binding.

Social agreements

The presumption that an agreement is not intended to be legally binding is also applied to social relationships between people who are not related. With both the above though, there can be exceptions.

Commercial agreements

There is a strong presumption in commercial agreements that the parties intend to be legally bound, and unless clear words are used this presumption stands. Where the words of a business agreement are ambiguous, the courts will favor the interpretation that suggests that the parties did intend to create legal relations.

The capacity to enter into a contract

The law states that individuals who enter into a contract must have the capacity to enter into a contract, otherwise it is voidable. Adults who have full capacity are able to enter into contracts and enforce them at law (unless they are illegal contracts).

The law sets out those who do not have legal capacity to contract, particularly providing special legal protection to those who are minors, or under a mental disability.

Minors and capacity in contract law

Individuals who are under the age of 18 are known as 'minors' under the Family Reform Act 1969. A minor can enter into a contract at law, however, such a contract is 'voidable' by the minor before they reach 18 (and for a time thereafter). This means that the minor can enforce the contract, but they can also terminate it if they wish. Once the minor reaches the age of 18, the contract becomes legally binding on both parties. However, there are exceptions to the general rule: a minor may need to enter into a contract to buy necessities, such as food, clothing, medicine and other things necessary for them and their lifestyle. Minors may also need to enter into legally binding contracts for their education, such as apprenticeships. These types of contract are enforceable against the minor, however, such contracts must be fair to be enforceable against the minor. So if a minor pays a reasonable price for items required in the circumstances, the minor is legally required to fulfil the contract (i.e. pay for the goods or service).

A case where such a contract has been enforced is that of *Doyle v White City Stadium* (1935), where there was an agreement to train a boxer. There was no money paid, but the contract was enforceable as it was considered that the contract was beneficial because of the training provided. Another case where the contract was held enforceable is *Clements v London & NW Rail Co* (1894) where certain benefits were removed following a contract of employment, but the contract was considered to be beneficial and was upheld.

When can a contract with minors be voided?

The courts may not uphold a contract if it is considered not to be to the benefit of the minor. For example, in the case of *De Francesco v Barnum* (1889), a minor aged 14 years old, entered into an agreement to train as a dancer on stage. However, the contract had conditions which were considered not beneficial to the minor and, therefore, the minor was not bound by the contact. More recently, in the 2006 case of *Proform Sports Management Ltd v Proactive Sports Management Ltd* the court had to consider a contract entered into by footballer Wayne Rooney (who was 17 at the time) with his agent. The High Court ruled that the contract was voidable because it was not an agreement equivalent to contracts of apprenticeship, education and service.

A 'voidable contract' is a contract that can be ended. The contract is still valid, but it can be avoided by the minor who can legally terminate the agreement – before reaching the age of 18 years, or within a reasonable time of coming of age. What is a reasonable time period will depend on the facts of the case. In the case of *Steinberg v Scala (Leeds) Ltd* (1923), the contract was voided because the minor was unable to keep up with payments. However, in the case of *Edwards v Carter* (1892) the court decided that the contract could not be rejected and the agreement was enforceable.

What happens if money has already been paid by a minor?

If money is paid by a minor under a contract, then usually this cannot be recovered unless it can be proved that the contract has not been beneficial to the minor. So if a minor enjoys goods or services, then seeks to terminate the contract and recover money already paid – he cannot be reimbursed.

In the case of *Pearce v Brain* (1929), a minor exchanged a motor cycle for a car, but found that the car had defects. The court decided that the contract must stand as he had used the car and, therefore, had enjoyed the benefit of it.

The Minors' Contracts Act 1987

This Act was introduced to protect minors alongside the common law (i.e. rulings of the courts). This Act also provides guarantees for minors contracting with adults. A contract is binding on the adult but not on the minor; however, if the minor ratifies the contract after having reaching the age of 18 by, for instance, an act confirming a promise made when a minor – he is legally bound.

Furthermore, the contact is not void while still a minor – and any money paid under the contract terms cannot be repaid unless there has been no benefit received.

However, there are exceptions, the most likely of which to arise is that of a contract for 'necessities' as discussed above.

Corporations

A corporation is a legal entity that is treated by law as having a separate identity from the persons who constitute it. There are three main types of corporation: registered companies, corporations established by statute and chartered corporations. Each has a different level of contracting ability.

Registered companies

These are companies registered under the Companies Act 2006, which superseded the 1985 Companies Act and which covers most commercial companies. When registering, companies must supply a document that regulates their activities called a memorandum of association, which contains information including an objects clause, laying down the range of activities that their company can engage in. Under the 1989 Companies Act, which has been replaced by the 2006 Act a company can be liable for a contract made outside its stated activities if the other party has acted in good faith.

Statutory companies

These corporations are created by an Act of Parliament, for specific purposes, the Independent Broadcasting Authority is an example, as are local authorities. The statute creating the particular corporation will specify the purposes for which that corporation may make contracts. Any contracted outside of these purposes is null and void.

Chartered corporations

These are corporations set up by Royal Charter, which means that their rights are officially granted by the Crown. Examples are charities and some universities and other educational institutions. They have the same contractual capacity as an adult human being.

Formalities

We have discussed the fact that an agreement, with some exceptions, does not have to take a specific written form in order to be deemed a binding contract. A contract can be oral. One famous recent case involving an oral contract was Hadley v Kemp (1990) where Gary Kemp was the songwriter in the group Spandau Ballet. He was sued by other members of the group for royalties received for the group's music. The basis of the claim was that there was an oral agreement to share royalties. They were unable to prove the existence of any oral agreement and their claim failed.

Contracts which must be made by deed

The Law of Property Act 1925 states that a contract for a lease of more than three years must be made by deed, which basically means that it must be put into a formal document, signed in front of witnesses.

Contracts which must be in writing

Some statutes lay down that certain types of contract must be in writing. Most contracts involving sales of land must be in writing, under the Law of Property Act 1989. Other contracts that need to be in writing are those involving the transfers of shares in a limited company (Companies Act 2006 bills of exchange; cheques and promissory notes (Bills of Exchange Act (1882); and regulated consumer credit agreements, such as hire purchase agreements (Consumer Credit Act 1974, as amended by the 2006 Consumer Credit Act).

Contracts which must be evidenced in writing

Contracts of guarantee (where one party guarantees the obligations of another, such as parents guaranteeing a sons or daughters overdraft) are required to be 'evidenced in writing'. Contracts for sale or disposition of land before 27th September 1989 are still covered by the old law prior to the Law of Property Act 1989. Evidenced in writing means that although the contract itself may not be a written one, there must be written evidence of the transaction. The evidence must have existed before one party tried to enforce the contract against the other, and it must be signed by the party against whom the contract is to be enforced.

Electronic contracts

Many transactions and other forms of trade are now conducted electronically. For example, most people will at least be familiar with, if not frequent users of, ATMs situated outside or inside banks. When a bank's customer withdraws money or uses an ATM for other purposes, an electronic transaction takes place. More and more business is now done electronically, often with the parties never physically meeting each other. Online shops, for example, allow potential customers to browse, select and purchase goods without ever asking a salesperson for advice or assistance. Negotiations, giving quotes or submitting tenders for work may all be done electronically and indeed are. A great deal of information is now passed electronically within organisations and from one organisation to another. This all raises a number of legal questions, specifically with regard to electronic contracts. Some of the most important issues include whether an electronic contract is valid, that is, whether it must comply with certain formalities, whether

48

electronic signatures are admissible as evidence of intent and agreement, and what law applies to an electronic contract (if it is between international parties). These issues are addressed overleaf.

Formalities of an electronic contract

Generally, as we have seen, contracts can take any number of forms. They can be by deed, in writing, evidenced in writing, oral, or implied from the conduct of the parties. Certain contracts, however, require a specific form, and will not be legal (though they may be equitable) if they fail to comply with the formalities. For example, as we have seen, a conveyance of land or any interest in land must, under s52 of the Law of Property Act 1925, be by deed, save for the exceptions listed in that section.

Other contracts are required to be in writing. So what form, if any, must an electronic contract take? The answer depends on the nature of the contract.

If writing is a requirement, do documents which are stored digitally on a computer hard drive comply? Schedule 1 to the Interpretation Act 1978 states: "'Writing' includes typing, printing, lithography, photography and other modes of representing or reproducing words in a visible form, and expressions referring to writing are construed accordingly." Since words stored digitally on a computer may be reproduced on a monitor or printed onto paper, it would appear that computer storage is covered by this definition. Nevertheless, individual cases may still have to be decided by the courts.

49

Electronic signatures

A signature is generally understood as evidence that the signatory approves of a document's contents. But does this ring true also for a person's name printed on a telex or fax, or reproduced in electronic mail? In *Good Challenger Navegante SA v Metalexportimport SA (2004)* the Court of Appeal held that for the purposes of s30 of the Limitation Act 1980 a typed name on a telex was a signature. The Court held that "...the typed name of the sender at the end of the telex not only identified the maker but led to the inference that he had approved the contents." This does not apply to all instances of typed names, however, and a formal contract with typed names at the end with spaces underneath where the parties are expected to write their names would be unlikely to fall within the reasoning given in the Good Challenger case.

Above all, the signature must be able to objectively show that the signatory, by signing or printing their name, approved of a document's contents and intended to be bound by them. It is irrelevant whether the contents have been read (unless there has been some misrepresentation). The courts confirmed in Mehta v J Pereira Fernandes SA (2006) that a person's name which is shown as part of an email address in the header of an email does not mean that the person intended to be legally bound by the contents of the email. The automatic insertion of an email address could not be considered as a signature. Under s7 of the Electronic Communications Act 2000 an electronic signature is anything in electronic form which:

- is incorporated into or otherwise logically associated with any electronic communication or electronic data, and
- is certified as such by the signatory

Such a signature is admissible in evidence for the purpose of establishing the authenticity, the integrity, or both, of the electronic communication or data.

Certification of the signature requires the signatory to make a statement that the signature, its production, communication or verification, or a procedure applied to it, is a valid means of establishing the authenticity, integrity or both of the electronic communication or data.

Contracts concluded electronically

Article 9 of Directive 2000/31/EC, on electronic commerce, requires EU member states to ensure both that contracts can be concluded by electronic means and that the law does not create any barriers against using such contracts or which deprive such contracts of their validity. In the UK, the Electronic Communications Act 2000 supports approved cryptography service providers and provides that electronic signatures are admissible in evidence. Some contracts, though, such as those which transfer rights in real estate, are exempt from these general principles. Article 10 of Directive 2000/31/EC requires certain information to be provided regarding electronic contracts, such as describing the technical steps to be followed to conclude the contract, and the technical means for identifying and correct input errors before placing orders.

Ch. 3

Consideration and Contracts

In this chapter we look at the notion of consideration which is central to contract law. We look at the different types of consideration

As we saw in chapter 2, English law states that a contract is not usually binding unless it is supported by consideration. Consideration is usually said to mean that each party to a contract must give something in return for what is gained from the other party. Very basically, if there is a dispute and you wish to enforce someone's promise to you, then you must prove that you gave something in return for that promise. The key case that defined 'consideration' is *Currie v Misa* (1875), which states that consideration can consist of a right, interest, profit, benefit, detriment or forbearance. There are two types of consideration: executed and executory, as described below.

Consideration may be goods or services, a thing or a service. Many problems concerning consideration arise not when a contract is made but when one or other of the parties to the contract seeks to modify it, such as paying a lower price than agreed or supplying a different good or service.

Promisor and Promisee

In most contracts, it is the case that two promises will be exchanged, so each party to the contract is promisor and promisee. In a contract case, the claimant will often be arguing that the defendant has broken the promise made to the claimant and therefore the claimant will usually be the promisee. One example is if A contracts to build a conservatory and B promises to pay £5000 for the conservatory, there are two promises in this contract. A's promise to build a conservatory and B's promise to pay. If A fails to build the conservatory B can sue him. If the issue of consideration arises, B will seek to prove that his promise to pay £5000 was consideration for A's promise for building the conservatory. In that action, A will be the promisor and B the promisee. However, reverse the situation and B fails to pay, then A will sue and, if consideration is at issue, A will have to prove that his promise to build the conservatory was consideration for B's promise to pay. In that action, A will be the promisee and B the promisor.

'Executory' and 'executed' consideration

As mentioned above, consideration can fall into two categories: executory and executed. Executed consideration is the performance of an act in return for a promise. Executory consideration is when the person makes a promise, and the other person offers a counter promise – you promise to deliver goods to me and I promise to pay for them when they arrive, the promise is executory because it is something to be done in the future.

Consideration must be given in return for the promise or act of the other party. Something done, given, or promised beforehand will not be counted as consideration. A classic case concerning this arose in *Roscorla v Thomas (1842)*. The defendant sold the plaintiff a horse. After the sale was completed, the defendant told the plaintiff that the animal was 'sound and free from any vice'. This was not the actual truth and the plaintiff sued. The court held that the defendants promise was unenforceable, because it was made after the sale. If the promise about the horse's condition had been made before, the plaintiff would have provided consideration for it by buying the horse. As it was made after the sale, the consideration was past, for it had not been given in return for the promise.

There are two exceptions to the rule that past consideration is no consideration. The first is where the past consideration was provided at the promisors request, and it was understood that payment would be made. The second is the bill of exchange. Under s27 of the Bills of Exchange Act 1882, an antecedent debt or 'liability' may be consideration for receipt of a bill of exchange.

The rules of consideration
Consideration need not be adequate
The law of contract regulates the making of bargains. As freedom of contract is vital, the law is not concerned with whether a party has made a good bargain or a bad one. Adequacy is given its normal meaning-the contract is enforceable even if the price does not match the value of what is being gained under the agreement. One such case that reflects this is *Thomas v Thomas (1842)*. Before he

died Thomas expressed a wish that his wife should be allowed to remain in his house although there was no mention of this in his will. The executors carried out his wish but charged the widow a nominal ground rent of £1 a year. When they later tried to dispossess her they failed.

Consideration must be sufficient

Consideration offered is sufficient provided that:

- It is real (White v Bluett (1853)
- It is tangible (Ward v Byham (1956)
- It has some discernible value (Chappel v Nestle (1960); and
- Economic value is measured against benefit gained.

Consideration must not be past

Consideration must follow rather than precede agreement. This prevents coercion by suppliers of goods and services.

Consideration must be of economic value

What this principle basically means is that there must be some physical value, rather than just an emotional or sentimental value.

Consideration can be a promise not to sue

If one party has a possible civil claim against the other, a promise not to enforce that claim is good consideration for a promise given in return. One clear example is if A crashes into B's car then A can promise not to sue if B pays for the damage.

Performance of an existing duty

Where a promisee already owes the promisor a legal duty, then in theory performing that duty should not in itself be consideration. If the promisee does nothing more than they are already obliged to do, they are suffering no detriment and the promisor is only getting a benefit to which he or she is entitled.

Existing duties can be divided into three categories: public duties; contractual duties to the promisor; and contractual duties to a third party.

Existing public duty

Where a person is merely carrying out duties they are legally bound to perform – such as police officer or juror, doing that alone will not be consideration. However, where a promisee is under a public duty, but does something beyond the call of that duty, that extra act amounts to consideration. In *Glasbrook Brothers v Glamorgan County Council (1925)* the owners of a South Wales Mine asked the police to place a guard at their colliery during a strike. The police suggested that regular checks by mobile patrol would be adequate but the owners replied that they wanted something more intensive and the police agreed at an extra cost of £2,200. After the strike the owners refused to pay saying that the police had a duty to protect their property. The courts held in favor of the police saying that the police did not have a duty to supply the cover they did, only the cover they deemed sufficient. Anything over and above was deemed consideration.

Existing contractual duty to the promisor

The position on contractual duties and consideration has changed from the traditional position whereby the performance of an existing contractual duty owed to a promisor was not consideration. In *Stilk v Myrick (1809)* two sailors deserted a ship during a voyage and the captain was unable to find replacements. The remaining crew-members were promised extra wages for sailing the ship back to London but the captain refused to pay on arrival and the sailors sued with the court holding that there was no consideration as the sailors had already contracted to sail the boat back to its destination.

In *Hartley v Ponsonby (1857)* half the crew deserted and the remaining crew were offered extra wages to carry on the journey. At the end the captain refused to pay and the crew sued and won, as the courts held that there was consideration as the crew were to small to sail the boat adequately and extra money was justified.

An exception to the rule that performance of an existing contractual obligation owed to the promisor will not amount to consideration will occur where a party can be seen to receive an extra benefit from the other party's agreement to carry out his existing obligations. One such case that highlights this is that of *Williams v Roffey Brothers (1991)*. In this case the defendants (the main contractors) were refurbishing a block of flats. They sub-contracted the carpentry works to the plaintiff. The plaintiff ran into financial difficulties, whereupon the defendants agreed to pay the plaintiff an additional sum if they completed the work on time. It was held that where a party to an existing contract later agrees to pay an 'extra bonus' in order that the other party performs his obligations under the original contract, then the new agreement is binding if the party agreeing to pay the bonus has thereby obtained some new practical advantage or avoided a disadvantage. In this particular case, the advantage was the avoidance of a penalty clause and the expense of finding new carpenters, among other factors.

Existing contractual duty to a third party

In some cases two parties make a contract to provide a benefit to a third party. If one of the parties (A) makes a further promise to that third party to provide the benefit they have already contracted to provide, that further promise can be good consideration for a promise made by the third party in return-even though nothing more than the contractual duty is being promised by A.

One case that illustrates this *is Scotson v Pegg (1861)*. Scotson contracted to supply a cargo of coal to a third party, X, or to anyone X nominated. Scotson was instructed by X to deliver the coal to Pegg, and Pegg promised to unload the coal at a stated rate of pay. He subsequently failed to do the agreed unloading. Scotson sued Pegg, claiming that their promise to deliver coal to him was consideration for his promise to unload it. Pegg claimed that this could not be consideration, since Scotson was already bound to supply the coal under the contract with X. The court upheld Scotson's claim: delivery of the coal was consideration because it was a benefit to Pegg, and a detriment to Scotson in that it prevented them from having the option of breaking their contract with X.

Waiver and Promissory estoppel

These are ways of making some kind of promise binding even where there is no consideration. Waiver has traditionally applied where one party agrees not to enforce their strict rights under the contract by, for example, accepting delivery later than agreed. One case that illustrates the doctrine of waiver is that of *Hickman v Haynes (1875)*. A buyer asked the seller to deliver goods later than originally agreed and then when the delivery was made refused to accept it. The seller sued for breach of contract, the buyer responded by arguing that the seller was in breach, for delivering later than specified. The courts rejected the buyer's argument on the grounds that the delivery was made at the buyer's request.

Promissory estoppel (stopping the contract on the basis of a promise) is a newer doctrine than waiver, developing the concept. It was introduced by Lord Denning in the *Central London Property Trust Ltd v High Trees (1947)* where owners of a block of flats had promised to accept reduced rents in 1939. There was no consideration for their promise but Lord Denning nevertheless stated that he would estop them from recovering any arrears. He based his case on the decision in *Hughes v Metropolitan Railways (1875)*. In this case, under the lease the tenants were obliged to keep the premises in good repair, and in October 1874, the landlord gave them six months notice to do some repairs stating that if they were not done in time, the lease would be forfeited. In November the two parties began to negotiate the possibility of the tenants buying the lease, the tenants stating in the meantime that they would not carry out the repairs. By December the negotiations had broken down and at the end of the six-month notice period, the landlord claimed that the lease was forfeited because the tenants had not done the repairs. The House of Lords (now Supreme Court) held however, that the landlord's conduct was an implied promise to the tenants that he would not enforce the forfeiture at the end of the notice period, and in not doing the repairs, the tenants had been relying on this premise. It was seen that the six-month notice period began again when negotiations broke down.

The exact scope of the doctrine is a matter of debate, but certain requirements must be met:

- Estoppel only applies to the modification of discharge of an existing contractual obligation. It cannot create a new contract.
- It can only be used as a 'shield' and not a 'sword'.
- The promise not to enforce rights must be clear and unequivocal.
- It must be inequitable for the promisor to go back on his promise.
- The promisee must have acted in reliance on the promise, although not necessarily to his detriment.

Agreement by deed

When is a deed required?

Land law, The Law of Property Miscellaneous Provisions Act1989, requires all transfers of land or the creation of interests in land, such as gifts or mortgages, to be made by way of legal deed, otherwise it is void as far as the legal estate is concerned. A document will be a deed if:

- It makes clear on the face of it that it is intended to be a deed;

- It is validly executed as a deed by all those required to sign it;

- It is validly executed as a deed by an individual if it is signed by the individual in the presence of a witness who attests to the signature, or at their direction and in their presence and the presence of two witnesses who each attest the signature, and it is delivered as a deed by them or a person authorised to do so on their behalf.

When is the transfer deed fully effective?

In registered land, the transfer deed is legally effected only when it is lodged at the Land Registry for registration on the official Registered Title of the property. If the transfer is of unregistered land, the transfer deed is effective immediately to vest the legal estate in the purchaser, but the transfer must be lodged for first registration of title with the Land Registry within 2 months (otherwise the seller will hold the legal estate on bare trust for the purchaser). However, the 2-month period can be extended with good reason.

Rights that are overreaching

A purchaser will take the property subject to the beneficial interests of anyone they knew or ought to have known about (under the doctrine of 'notice'). A typical example is where the purchaser buys land subject to a trust, knowing that an individual has a life interest in the property and can remain in occupation until their death.

Overreaching is a process whereby the beneficiaries' equitable interests are effectively dissolved and lifted from the land, and then attached to the purchase price. The purchaser then takes the land free from the beneficiaries' equitable interests, whether or not he knew or ought to have known of them, and the beneficiary claims his entitlement from the money made through the selling of the property.

When does overreaching apply?

Overreaching is capable of applying only to the equitable interests listed in section 2 Law of Property Act 1925. These are generally those existing behind a trust and having a monetary value. Section 2(1) LPA 1925 provides that: "A conveyance to a purchaser of a legal estate in land shall overreach any equitable interest or power affecting that estate [and listed in the section] whether or not he has notice thereof."

Generally speaking, for overreaching to be effective the purchaser (which includes a mortgagee) must pay the purchase money/mortgage loan to all of the trustees (at least two, or a trust corporation). Provided this is done, the purchaser/mortgagee takes free of any beneficial interests existing behind a trust. The beneficiaries' equitable interests are then lifted from the land and automatically attached to the money paid by the purchaser (i.e. to the proceeds of sale).

Ch. 4

Terms of Contracts

In this chapter we look at the main terms of contracts and what must be inherent in a contract before it can be legally binding. Express terms of contract and implied terms are examined along with collateral agreements and unfair contract terms. Finally, we look at misrepresentation, duress and undue influence. Illegality of contract is dealt with in chapter 6.

Once a contract has been formed, it is necessary to define the scope of the obligations which each party incurs. Terms of contracts describe the respective duties and obligations of each party to the contract. As well as the contractual terms laid out and agreed by parties to a contract, called express terms, there may also be implied terms – terms that are 'read into' a contract because of the facts of the agreement and the apparent intention of the parties or the law on specific types of contract.

Express terms of contract

Oral statements

In all transactions, with the exception of the simplest, there will be some negotiations before a contract is made. These are usually oral statements or based on oral statements. Problems can arise following oral statements when parties cannot agree whether the statement was intended to be binding. In considering questions such as these a court will classify statements made during negotiations as either representations or terms. A representation is a statement that may have encouraged one of the parties to make the contract, but is not itself part of the contract, while a term is an undertaking that is part of the contract.

Representation can also be construed as misrepresentation, which is a common cause of dispute. Whether a statement is either a representation or a term is mainly a question of the party's intentions. If the parties have indicated that a particular statement is a term of their contract, then the court will carry out that intention.

Written terms of a contract

Written terms can be incorporated into a contract in three different ways: by signature, by reasonable notice and by a previous course of dealing.

The parol evidence rule

Under this rule, where there is a written contract, extrinsic (parol) evidence cannot change the express terms laid down in that document. Extrinsic evidence includes oral statements and written material such as draft contracts or letter, whether relating to pre-contract negotiations or the parties post contractual behavior. One case that illustrates the parol evidence rule is *Henderson v Arthur (1907)*. The plaintiffs and the defendant were parties to a lease that contained a covenant for the payment of rent quarterly in advance, although before the lease was drawn up the parties agreed that the rent could be paid in arrears. When the tenant was sued for not paying quarterly in advance, he pointed out this prior agreement. The court held that the terms of prior oral agreement could not be substituted for the terms of a later formal contract covering the same transaction. There are a few exceptions to the parol evidence rule, the following being the main ones:

Rectification

Where a document is intended to record a previous oral agreement but fails to do that accurately, evidence of the oral agreement will be admitted.

Partially written agreements

Where there is a written agreement, but the parties clearly intended it to be qualified by other written or oral statements, the parol evidence rule is displaced.

Implied terms

The parol evidence rule only applies where a party seeks to use existing evidence to alter the express terms of a contract. Where a contract is of a type that is unusually subject to terms implied by law and statute, parol evidence may be given to support, or to deny, the usual implication.

*

Collateral agreements

There is a way in which an oral statement can be deemed binding, even though it conflicts with a written contract and does not fall within any of the exceptions to the parol rule. If one party says something like 'I will sign this document if you will assure me that it means....' The courts may find that two contracts have been created, the written agreement and a collateral contract based on the oral statement.

Construction of express terms in contracts

The courts will sometimes have to determine the construction of an express term within a contract. The courts will have to 'seek the meaning which the document would convey to a reasonable person having all the background knowledge which would have reasonably been available to parties at the time of entering into the agreement'. The courts start by presuming that the parties meant what they said. The courts would also look at the outcome of the words and meaning to see if they create an absurdity or are inconsistent with the rest of the contract.

Implied terms

As well as the express terms laid down in the contract, further terms may be sometimes read into the contract by the courts. These implied terms are divided into four groups: terms implied by fact, terms implied by law, terms implied by custom and terms implied by trade usage. Terms implied by fact are terms not laid out in the contract, but which it is assumed both parties would have intended to include if they had thought about it, they may have left them out by mistake. In order to decide what the intention of the parties was, the courts have developed two tests, the 'officious bystander test, and the 'business efficacy' test.

The officious bystander test was laid down in *Shirlaw v Southern Foundries (1926)*. The Judge said, ...'that which in any contract is left to be implied and need not be expressed is something so obvious that it goes without saying: so that, if while the parties were making their bargain, an officious bystander were to suggest some express provision for it in the agreement, they would testily suppress him with a common 'oh, of course'. The business efficacy test covers terms which one side alleges must be implied to make the contract work, to give it business efficacy.

Terms implied by law are terms which the law dictates must be present in certain types of contract-in some cases whether the parties intended them or not.

In *Liverpool Council v Irwin (1977)* the defendants lived in a council maisonette that was part of a high-rise block in Liverpool. The block was in a bad condition and tenants withheld rent and the case went to court with the tenants arguing that the council was in breach of contract (tenancy). The council argued that there was no agreement to keep the block in good condition and the courts argued that good repair and safety were implied terms of contract. The council lost the case.

Other implied terms may arise from contracts governing the supply of goods and services, such as the Consumer Rights Act 2015. Terms implied by custom can be implied into a contract if there is evidence that under local custom they would normally be there. Terms implied by trade usage would normally be part of a contract made by parties in a particular trade or business.

The classification of contractual terms

There are three types of contractual terms, conditions, warranties and innominate terms. A condition is a term that the courts would regard as important in that it would clearly have negative consequences if breached.

Where a condition is breach the injured party can regard the contract as repudiated, and need not render any further performance, and can also sue for damages.

Warranties denote contractual terms that can be broken without highly important consequences. This would be a minor term and would not entitle the party to terminate the contract it merely entitles him to sue. The Consumer Rights Act 2015 designates certain terms as warranties breach of which does not allow the buyer to treat the contract as discharged, but merely to sue for damages, for example, the right to quiet enjoyment.

One such case that illustrates the above is that of *Bettini v Gye (1876)* where a singer was engaged to sing for a whole season and to arrive six days in advance to take part in rehearsals. He arrived only three days in advance. It was held that the rehearsal clause was a warranty, as it was subsidiary to the main clause. The management were therefore not entitled to treat the contract as discharged. They should have kept to the original contract and sought damages for the three days delay.

Innominate terms are terms that can be broken with either important or trivial consequences, depending on the nature of the breach.

Innominate terms were illustrated in *Hong Kong Fir Shipping Co Ltd v Kawasaki Kisen Kaisha (1962)* in which the defendants had chartered a ship for two years from the claimants. Twenty weeks of the charter were lost due to condition of ship and incompetent staff. The agreement contained a clause stating that the ship was 'in every way fitted for ordinary cargo service'. There was no doubt that the defendants were entitled to bring an action for damages but instead decided to terminate the contract. The claimants counter sued, claiming that the breach did not entitle the defendants to terminate, only to claim damages. The Court of Appeal agreed, stating that the question to be asked was that whether as a result of the breach the defendants had been deprived of the whole of the benefit of the contract. As this was not the case, the termination was unjustified.

Unfair contract terms

Contract terms can be considered to be so unfair to one of the contracting parties that the courts have had to intervene to prevent an injustice. This has usually arisen within the context of exemption clauses and is controlled both by common law and the exemption clauses in contracts. Parts 1 and 2 of the Consumer Rights Act 2015 consolidate and replace the Unfair Terms in Consumer Contracts Regulations 1999 (UTCCRs) and relevant provisions of the Unfair Contract Terms Act 1977 (UCTA).

The Unfair Contract Terms Act 1977 applies only to exemption clauses covering business liability and, since the CRA 2015, does not cover any exemption clauses that would be covered by the Act, i.e. in contracts between a trader and a consumer. The Act defines a 'trader' as a person acting for purposes relating to that persons trade, business craft or profession. A 'consumer' is defined as an individual acting for purposes that are wholly or mainly outside the indiviual's trade, business, craft or profession *(see Overy v Paypal (Europe) Ltd 2012.*

In certain cases, one party to a contract may seek to avoid incurring liabilities for breach of contract, or may specify that their liability for such a breach will be limited, usually to a specific amount of damages. However, a clause that seeks to exclude all liability for uncertain breaches is called an exclusion clause. There are many examples such as holiday companies seeking to exclude all liability for holidays gone wrong or cancelled. Over the past 40 years the law has sought to control the use of these clauses, first by the efforts of judges and also by legislation such as the Unfair Contract Terms Act 1977 and the Unfair Terms in Consumer Contracts Regulations 1999, now consolidated as described above by the CRA 2015.

Misrepresentation in contracts

Even in cases where a contract clearly meets the requirements of offer and acceptance, consideration and intent to create legal relations, it will still not be binding if, at the time the contract was made, certain factors were present which meant that there was no genuine concern. These are known as vitiating factors (because they vitiate, or invalidate, consent). The vitiating factors that the law recognizes as preventing a contract are misrepresentation, mistake, duress, undue influence and illegality. In these cases, the innocent party may set the contract aside if he wishes. If one party has been induced to enter into a contract by a statement made by the other party, and that statement is untrue, the contract is voidable and the innocent party may also be able to claim damages. For a misrepresentation to be actionable it must be untrue, a statement of fact not opinion, and it must have induced the innocent party to enter into the contract.

It is worth noting that, following the amendments to the Consumer Protection from Unfair Trading Regulations 2008 (CPRs 2008) made by the Consumer Protection Amendment Regulations 2014, after October 1st 2014 consumers who entered into a contract for the sale or supply of a product by a trader or who entered into a contract to sell a product to a trader (for example selling a car to a dealer) or made a payment to a trader for the supply of a product, and that trader engaged in a prohibited practice in relation to that product, for example by giving misleading information, have an extended range of specific consumer 'rights to redress' under the CPRs (right to unwind, right to a discount, and specific rights to damages). This regime is separate to the consumers general remedies but the consumer cannot make a claim twice for the same product. In addition, there is an amendment to s.2 of the Misrepresentation Act 1967 which removes the ability of consumers to recover damages under that legislation where they have a right to redress under the CPRs in respect of the misrepresentation,

There are four different types of misrepresentation, fraudulent misrepresentation, where there is clear deceit, negligent, where misrepresentation arises through acts of negligence but not deceit and innocent misrepresentation which is not fraudulent but is still clear misrepresentation. The effect of a misrepresentation is generally to make a contract voidable, rather than void, so the contract will continue to exist unless or until the injured party chooses to have it set aside by the courts by means of rescission. Rescission is an equitable remedy that sets the contract aside and puts the parties back in the position where they were before the misrepresentation. An injured party who decides to rescind the contract may do so by notifying the other party or, if this is not possible owing to the conduct of the party, by taking some reasonable action to indicate the intention to default.

A case that illustrates this is *Car and Universal Finance Co Ltd v Caldwell (1965)* where the defendant sold and delivered a car and was paid by cheque. The cheque bounced, by which time the car and buyer had disappeared. The defendant notified the police and the Automobile Association. While the police were investigating the buyer sold the car to a dealer who knew that the car was not the buyer's to sell. Finally, the car dealer sold the car to the claimants who bought it in good faith. The Court of Appeal held that by contacting the police and the AA the claimant had made his intention to rescind the contract clear. As soon as this happened the ownership of the car reverted to him. This meant that at the time the car was sold back to the claimant the car was not anyone's to sell.

Another case illustrating this is *Whittington v Seale-Hayne (1900)* where the plaintiff's, breeders of prize poultry, were induced to take a lease of the defendant's premises by his innocent representation that the premises were in a sanitary condition. Under the lease, the plaintiff's covenanted to execute any works required by any local or public authority. Owing to the insanitary conditions of the premises, the water supply was poisoned, the plaintiff's manager and his family became very ill, and the poultry became valueless for breeding purposes or died.

The court rescinded the lease, and held that the plaintiffs could recover an indemnity for what they had spent on rates, rent and repairs under the covenants in the lease, because these expenses arose necessarily out of the contract. It refused to award compensation for other leases, since to do so would be to award damages, not an indemnity, there being no obligation created by the contract to carry on a poultry farm on the premises or to employ a manager, etc.

Representation and terms of a contract

Section 1 of the Misrepresentation Act 1967, s.2 as amended by The Consumer Protection Amendment Regulations 2014, described above, provides that where a misrepresentation becomes a term of the contract, the innocent party may bring an action for both misrepresentation and breach of contract. Under section 3 of this Act, as amended by the Unfair Contract Terms Act 1977, as amended by the CRA 2015, exemption clauses that attempt to exclude or limit liability for misrepresentations are operative only if reasonable. This provision is illustrated in *Walker v Boyle (1982)* where the seller of a house told the buyer that there were no disputes regarding the boundaries of the property. This was not true. This misrepresentation appeared to entitle the buyer to rescind the contract and notwithstanding a clause seeking to deny this, the court granted a rescission.

Mistake

The general rule is that a mistake has no effect on a contract, but certain mistakes of a fundamental nature, sometimes called operative mistakes, may render a contract void at common law. If the contract is rendered void, then the parties will be returned to their original positions, and this may defeat the rights of innocent third parties who may have acquired an interest in the contract.

The reluctance of the courts to develop the common law doctrine of mistake is probably due to the unfortunate consequences for third parties that can result from holding a contract void. Equity at one stage intervened to create a more flexible doctrine, but this has been overruled. We discuss mistakes in more depth in the next chapter.

Rectification

Where there has been a mistake, not in the actual agreement but in reducing it in writing, equity will order rectification of the document so that it coincides with the true agreement of the parties.

74

The main conditions for this are that:

- The document does not represent the intention of both parties; or
- One party mistakenly believes that a term was included in the document and the other party knew of this error.
- There must have been a concluded agreement but not necessarily an enforceable contract. Rectification is an equitable remedy and is available at the discretion of the court.

Refusal of specific performance

Specific performance will be refused when the contract is void at common law. Equity may also refuse specific performance where a contract is valid at law, but only 'where a hardship amounting to injustice would have been inflicted upon him by holding him to his bargain' *(Tamplin v James (1879))*.

Duress

This requires actual or threatened violence to the person. Originally, it was the only form of duress recognized by the law. This is highlighted by the case of *Barton v Armstrong (1975)* where a managing director was threatened with death if he did not purchase a former chairman's shares. The managing director was happy to purchase the shares notwithstanding the threats that had been made. It was held that the threats constituted duress and the contract was set aside. We will look at duress in more depth in chapter 7.

Ch. 5

Errors and Contracts

In this chapter we look at the effect that an error or errors in a contract has on the parties involved. We take a look at general principles and common mistakes and also rectification.

The general rule is that a mistake has no effect on a contract, but certain mistakes of a fundamental nature, sometimes called operative mistakes can render a contract void at common law.. However, the law in this area operates quite rigidly.

The general principles

There are four types of mistake within contract law, Common mistake, unilateral mistake, mutual mistake and mistake relating to identity. All are underpinned by general rules. There is an objective principle, or test that the court will apply when considering mistakes within contracts. The courts do not ask the parties to the contract what they thought they were entering into but rather they consider what an onlooker would have thought it was each party was agreeing to. This is very much akin to the 'officious bystander test' referred to earlier. Another key principle is that in order to void a contract the mistake must be made before the contract is completed. One case that illustrates this is _Amalgamated_

Investment and Property Co Ltd v John Walker and sons Ltd (1977). In this case, a contract was made for the sale of a warehouse, for £1,710,000. The sellers knew that the purchasers were buying the warehouse with the intention of redeveloping it. The day after the contract was signed, the Department of the Environment, as it was then, made the property a listed building. This made it more difficult for the buyers to get permission to redevelop. Without this permission the warehouse would be worth considerably less. Neither party to the contract had been aware that the DOE were going to list the building.

The Court of Appeal held that the contract was valid as at the time of the agreement both parties were perfectly correct in their belief that the building was not listed, so there was no operative mistake. In the past, only a mistake of fact could negate a contract not a mistake of law. However, in the light of certain key cases, this is not now the case.

Common mistake

Having explored the general principles underpinning the treatment of mistakes in contract it is now time to explore the types of mistake more thoroughly.

Common mistakes are also known as identical mistakes, shared mistake or mistake nullifying consent. In this situation both parties make the same mistake-for example if A buys an antique from B which both parties think is rare and valuable, such as Wedgwood Pottery, but which is in fact a fake, they have made a shared mistake which would only render the contract void if the mistake relates to one of three subjects which the courts consider fundamental to the contract: the existence of the subject matter, its ownership and, in limited cases, its quality. A mistake as to the existence of subject matter will usually only concern goods to be sold-if for example A purports to sell a motorbike to B, and it is then discovered that the motorbike has been destroyed by fire, the contract will not be valid. It can apply equally to other subject matter. The main test is, do the goods or other exist at the time of a contract?

One case that illustrates this is *Scott v Coulson (1993)*. A life insurance policy was taken out, covering a person's death. In fact the person was already dead so the contract was null and void.

It is not always the case that the non-existence of subject matter will render the contract null and void. There have been several cases that obscure this general principle. One such case was *Couturier v Hastie (1856)* that involved a contract to buy a cargo of corn, which, at the time the contract was made was supposed to be on a ship sailing to England from the Mediterranean port of Salonica. In fact by that time the corn had already been sold by the master of the ship to a buyer in Tunis because the corn had started to deteriorate and go off. This is a common occurrence and the master's action was the usual accepted solution. For the purposes of the original contract the corn had ceased to exist. The sellers claimed that the buyers still had an obligation to pay as per the contract. The House of Lords held that the buyer did not have to pay for the corn, as the goods did not exist. There was no mistake; quite simply the corn did not exist.

Mistake as to title

Very rarely, a situation will arise in which one party agrees to transfer property to the other but unknown to both parties, the latter already owns that property. In such a case, the contract will be void for mistake. This is obviously very rare but has happened on occasion.

Mistaken identity

There is a presumption that a contract is valid even where one party has made a mistake as to the identity of the other. However, this presumption can be denied or negated by the party who has made the mistake. If this is done the contract is void at common law. In order to achieve this the mistaken party must prove that they intended to deal with a person other than the person who was in fact the other party to the contract, and that the identity of the other party was regarded as of fundamental importance.

One key case that illustrates this is *Cundy V Lindsey (1878)*. The claimants received an order for a large number of handkerchiefs from a Mr Blenkarn of 37 Wood Street, Cheapside. Mr Blenkarn rented a room at that address, and further down the road at 123 Cheapside, were the offices of a firm called Blenkiron and Co. Blenkarn signed his name so it looked liked Blenkiron. The claimants sent off their goods addressed to Blenkiron and Co. Mr Blenkarn received them and by the time that the fraud was discovered he had sold them to the defendants, Cundy, who had bought them in good faith. The claimants sued the defendants to get the money back, and their success in this depended on whether it could be proved

80

that there was a contract between the claimants and Blenkarn. The House of Lords held that there was no contract between Blenkarn and the claimants, because they had intended all along to deal with Blenkiron and Co. The court very importantly held that 'between him and them there was no consensus of mind which could lead to...any contract whatsoever.

Mistake over the terms of the contract

Where one party is mistaken as to the terms of the contract, and the other knows this, the contract will be void, regardless of whether the term is fundamental.

Mistakes relating to documents

Where a mistake relates to a written document there are two special remedies in existence, *non est factum* and rectification. Although the general principle is that a contract becomes effective when a person signs it, regardless of whether they understood it, *non est factum* (this is not my deed) becomes operative where a person signs a document believing it to be something totally different from what it actually was. This remedy may make the contract void. In order to void the contract the person seeking this remedy must prove three things: that the signature was induced by a trick or a fraud, that they made a fundamental mistake as to the nature of the document and that they were not careless in signing it. The mistake made by the signee must concern the actual nature of the contract and not just its legal effect.

Mutual and unilateral mistakes

These mistakes negate consent, that is they prevent the formation of an agreement. The courts adopt an objective test in deciding whether agreement has been reached. It is not enough for one of the parties to allege that he was mistaken. Mistake can negate consent in the following cases.

Mutual mistakes concerning the identity of the subject matter

In these cases the parties are at cross-purposes, but there must have been some ambiguity in the situation before the courts will declare the contracts void.

One such case that illustrates this is *Raffles v Wichelhaus (1864)* where a consignment of cotton was bought to arrive on the ship *Peerless* from Bombay. Two ships, both called Peerless, were due to leave Bombay at around the same time. It was held that there was no agreement as the buyer was thinking of one ship and the seller was referring to the other ship.

Unilateral mistake concerning the terms of the contract

Here, one party has taken advantage of the other party's error. In *Hartog v Colin and Shields (1939)* the sellers mistakenly offered to sell goods at a given price per pound when they intended to offer them per piece. All the preliminary negotiations had been on a per piece basis. The buyers must have realised that the sellers had made a mistake. It was held that the contract was void.

Unilateral mistakes as to the identities of other parties to the contract

Where the identity of the other party is of fundamental importance, and there has been a genuine mistake, the contract will be void. In Cundy v Lindsey (1878), as mentioned above, a Mr Blenkarn ordered goods from Lindsey signing the letter to give the impression that the order came from Blenkiron and Co, a firm known as Lindsey and Co. It was held that the contract was void. Lindsey and Co had only intended to do business with Blenkiron and Co. there was therefore a mistake concerning the identity of the other party to the contract.

A mistake as to attributes or credit-worthiness will not render a contract void. In *Kings Norton Metal Co v Edridge Merrett and Co Ltd (1872)* a Mr Wallis ordered goods on impressive stationary which indicated that the order had come from Hallam and Co, an old established firm with branches all over the country. It was held that the contract was not void. The sellers intended to do business with the writer of the letter; they were merely mistaken as to his attributes, that is, the size and credit worthiness of his business.

Another case illustrating this is *Boulton v Jones (1857)* where the defendant sent an order for some goods to a Mr Brocklehurst unaware that he had sold his business to his foreman, the plaintiff. The plaintiff supplied the goods but the defendant refused to pay for them as he had only intended to do business with Brocklehurst, against whom he had a set off. It was held that there was a mistake concerning the identity of the other party and the contract was therefore void.

Mistake in equity

The narrow approach taken by the common law towards remedies for mistake (that is that it renders the contract void) is supplemented by the more flexible approach of equity. The following remedies may be available in equity: rescission (discussed above); rectification and refusal of specific performance.

Rectification

Where some aspect of a written document is alleged not to reflect accurately the will of the parties, the remedy of rectification may in certain instances allow the written document to be altered so that it coincides with the true agreement of the parties. In order for this remedy to be applied, three conditions must be satisfied: the parties must have agreed about the point in question; the agreement on that aspect of the contract must have continued unchanged up to the time it was put into writing and the written document must fail to express the parties agreement on that point.

****

Ch. 6

Contracts And Illegality

In this chapter we look at the concept of legally unenforceable contracts and the effect of this on parties to a contract .We also look at modes of performance and breaches of common law and legislation generally, plus contracts prejudicial to public safety.

Although a contract, on the face of it may contain all the elements of a valid agreement, such as offer and consideration, that contract may still be legally unenforceable. Contracts may be illegal at the time of their formation or because of the way they have been performed. A contract may be illegal when entered into because the contract cannot be performed in accordance with its terms without committing an illegal act. For example, a contract may involve a breach of the criminal law, or it may be a statutory requirement for the parties to the contract to have a license that they in fact do not have. A case that illustrates this is *Levy v Yates (1838)*. In this case, there existed a statutory rule that a royal license was required to perform a play within 20 miles of London. In that case the contract was between a theatre owner and an impresario for the performance of a theatrical production where no royal license had been obtained. The contract was thus illegal at the time of its formation.

Illegal mode of performance

In some cases a contract may be perfectly legal when it was made, but may be carried out in an illegal manner. A case that illustrates this is *Anderson Ltd v Daniel (1924)*. In this case, a statute provided that a seller of artificial fertilizer had to supply buyers with an invoice detailing certain chemicals used in its manufacture. The sellers failed to provide the invoice needed. Although not against the law to sell fertilizer it was against statutory rules not to supply an invoice. As a result the sellers were unable to claim the price when the defendants refused to pay. A contract is obviously illegal if it involves a contravention of the law. However, a contract is also regarded as being illegal where it involves conduct that the law disapproves of as contrary to the interests of the public, even though the conduct is not actually unlawful. In both cases the transaction is treated as an illegal contract and the courts will not enforce it.

Contracts violating legal rules

Breach of common law

There are a number of factors that may make a contract illegal at common law, the most important where there is a contract to commit a crime or tort (negligent act). These are obvious breaches of the law. However, another very important area is contracts in restraint of trade. The issue of restraint of trade commonly arises and concerns those contracts that limit an individuals right to use their skills for payment, or to trade freely.

These contracts fall into four groups:

- Contracts for the sale of a business where the vendor promises not to compete with the purchaser
- Contracts between businesses by which prices or output are regulated
- Contracts in which an employee agrees that on leaving employment they will not set up in business or be employed in such as way as to compete with their employer or ex employer. This is most common in business where personal skills and reputation attract custom, such as advertising and the ex-employee may take with them valuable customers
- Contracts where a person agrees to restrict their mode of trade by, for example, only accepting orders from one particular company. This is sometimes called a 'solus' agreement and is frequently used for petrol stations, in return for the land or lease the trader promises to use the product of the seller (*Esso Petroleum v Harper's Garage (Stourport) 1968*).

Any of the above can be held to create a restraint of trade, a general restraint if the contract completely prohibits trading, or a partial restraint if it limits trading to a certain time or area.

Breach of legislation

Some types of contract are expressly declared void by statute. The two most important examples of contracts that are expressly declared void by statute are contracts in constraint of trade and wagering contracts.

Contracts in restraint of trade

As stated above, these are arrangements by which one party agrees to limit his or her legal right to carry out a trade, business or profession. A contract that does this is always viewed as *prima facie* void for two reasons:

- To prevent people signing away their livelihoods at the request of a party with stronger bargaining power
- To avoid depriving the public of the person's expertise.

These contracts are of several possible types as mentioned above- employee restraints, vendor restraints-preventing the seller of a business from unfairly competing with the purchaser and agreements of mutual regulation between businesses. However, these agreements might be upheld as reasonable:

- as between the parties-so the restraint must be no wider than to protect a legitimate interest
- in the public interest-so the restraint must not unduly limit public choice.

The reasonableness of the restraint is also measured against factors such as duration and geographical extent.

Employee restraints

An employer can legitimately protect trade secrets and client connection, but not merely prevent the employee from exercising his or her trade or skill. Reasonableness is measured against certain criteria:

A restraint in a highly specialised business is more likely to be reasonable.. In *Forster and Sons Ltd v Suggett (1918)* - court held that a restraint of 5 years on an employee from engaging in glass or glass bottle manufacturing was reasonable given the time and money invested into their training. *Nordenfelt v Maxim Nordenfelt Guns and Ammunition Co Ltd (1894)* - the court held that a term prohibiting Nordenfelt from starting a competing business anywhere in the world for 25 years was reasonable.

Pursuant to the Nordenfelt principle, restraint of trade clauses are void and unenforceable unless they are reasonable by reference to the interests of the parties and the public. The restraint must also be reasonable in terms of time and space. 3 Restraint of an employee in a key position is more likely to be reasonable.

An employer is not entitled to protect itself against the use of the skill and knowledge which the employee acquired during his or her employment. Those belong to the employee, who must be free to exploit them in the market place. Neither can an employer seek protection from competition per se since it is against the public interest that employees should be deprived of the opportunity to earn their living or to use their personal skills to the ultimate benefit of the community as a whole:

Herbert Morris Limited v Saxelby
[1916] AC 688.

Instead the employer must demonstrate that the covenant protects a legitimate business interest. In the Herbert Morris case, Lord Parker defined this as "some proprietary right, whether in the nature of a trade connection or in the nature of trade secrets, for the protection of which such a restraint is reasonably necessary". The concept was further developed by Lord Wilberforce in *Stenhouse Australia Limited v Phillips [1974] 1 All ER 117,* who said:

"The employer's claim for protection must be based on the identification of some advantage or asset inherent in the business which can properly be regarded as, in a general sense, his property, and which it would be unjust to allow the employee to appropriate for his own purposes, even though he (the employee) may have contributed to its creation".

In other words, the employer is entitled to prevent the employee taking unfair advantage of confidential information and business connections to which he had access in the course of his/her employment.

An employee may be significant to the business without even being a member of staff as demonstrated in Leeds rugby Ltd v Harris (2005). The duration of the extent must not be too long *(Home Counties Dairies v Skilton (1970)* and the geographical extent too wide *(Fitch v Dewes (1921).* Similarly, the range of activities that the restraint covers must be no wider than is necessary to protect legitimate interests *(J A Mont (UK) Ltd v Mills (1993)*.

Soliciting of clients can be prevented by such clauses, if not too wide *(M&S Drapers v Reynolds (1957*
). Also, including clients not within the original scope of the restraint is not unreasonable *(Hanover Insurance Brokers Ltd and Christchurch Insurance Brokers Ltd v Shapiro (1994)*. Attempting a restraint by other means is also void, including making contractual benefits subject to a restraint *(Bull v Pitney Bowes Ltd (1966)* and restraints in rules of associations *(Eastham v Newcastle United FC Ltd (1963)*.

Vendor restraints

These are void for public policy to prevent an individual from negotiating away his or her livelihood and also because the public may lose a valuable service. Restraints are more likely to be upheld as reasonable since businesses deal on more equal bargaining strength, even is restraint is very wide *(Nordenfelt v Maxim Nordenfelt Co (1894)*. The restraint must still protect a legitimate interest to be valid *(British Concrete Ltd v Schelff (1921)*.

Agreements between merchants, manufacturers or other trades

If the object is regulation of trade then they are void unless both sides benefit (English Hop Growers v Dering (1928). So they are void when the parties have unequal bargaining strength *(Schroder Publishing Co Ltd v Macaulay (1974)*-unless public policy dictates otherwise: Panayiotou v Sony Music International (UK) Ltd (1994).

Wagering contracts

Wagering agreements are bets, and were rendered void by The Gaming Act 1845 which remained in force until the Gambling Act 2005, which came into force in stages to 2007. The Act provides:

"All contracts or agreements, whether by parole or in writing, by way of gaming or wagering, shall be null and void, and no suit shall be brought or maintained in a court of law or equity for recovering any sum of money or valuable thing alleged to be won upon any wager..."

The Act does not make wagering agreements illegal it simply provides that neither party to such an agreement can legally enforce it. For the provisions of the legislation to apply, a wagering contract must be one in which there are two parties and the terms of the agreement are such that one party wins and the other loses. This means that football pools, for example, are not covered as its promoters take a percentage of the stake money and so gain by the transaction regardless of whether players win as well. The Act also covers gaming, which is defined by the Betting, Gaming and lotteries act 1963 as 'the playing of a game of chance for winnings in money or money's worth'. Games of chance include games that depend partly on skill and partly on chance. Athletic games and sports are excluded.

*

Competition law

Common law lays down certain controls on contracts in constraint of trade. These controls give only limited protection and actual legislation provides more adequate protection. One of the main goals of the European Union, through Article 85, is to promote free trade between member states and clearly restrictive trade can affect this policy. Where a restrictive trade agreement could affect trade between member states it will only be valid if allowed under both EU and English law.

In terms of contracts in English law, the relevant legislation is now contained in the Competition Act 1998 Along with the Enterprise Act 2002. This Act prohibits a number of anti-competitive practices. The 1998 Act applies to agreements between undertakings, decisions by associations of undertakings or concerted practices that (a) may affect trade and (b) have as their object or effect the prevention, restriction or distortion of trade. For the Act to prohibit an agreement the effect of the agreement must be significant and not minor.

Contracts against public policy

There exist a wide-range of contracts that are considered to be illegal because they are against public policy. As we discussed, public policy really means the interest of society at large and the contract must contravene it. Contracts promoting sexual immorality for example are seen as contravening public policy.

One case that illustrates this is *Armhouse Lee Ltd v Chappell (1996)* concerning a contract under which the defendants paid the plaintiffs to place adverts for telephone sex lines in magazines. When regulation concerning such publicity was tightened the defendants terminated the contract, as they no longer wished to advertise their services in this way. The plaintiffs brought an action for the money due under the contract and the defendants argued that the contract was illegal and unenforceable as it promoted sexual immorality. This defense was rejected by the Court of Appeal. The court held that though the adverts were distasteful the sex lines were generally accepted by society and were regulated by the telephone industry. There was no evidence, in the eyes of the Court of Appeal that any 'generally accepted moral code' condemned these telephone sex lines. It considered that contracts should only be found illegal under this heading if an element of public harm clearly existed.

Contracts prejudicial to public safety
The main types of contracts found illegal on these grounds are contracts with those living in an enemy country, contracts to perform acts which are illegal in a friendly foreign country and contracts which are damaging to foreign relations.

The effect of an illegal contract
The effect of an illegal contract will depend on whether it is illegal due to a statute or due to the common law. Where the contract is illegal due to a statute, in some cases the statute provides for the consequences of any illegality. Under common law an illegal contract is void and courts will not order it to be performed. The

precise effects of an illegal contract depend on whether the contract is illegal at the time of formation or is illegal due to the way in which it was performed. Contracts illegal at the time of formation are treated as if they were never made, so the illegal contract is unenforceable by either party. Contracts illegal as performed are slightly different as to their effect. It will be possible to enforce the illegal contract if the illegal act was merely incidental to the performance of the contract. For example, a contract for the delivery of goods may not be tainted by illegality when the lorry driver is caught speeding or under the influence of drink. Where the contract is merely illegal because of the way it was performed, it is possible for either both or only one of the parties to intend illegal performance. If both parties are aware that a contracts performance is illegal, the consequences for this type of contract are the same as for a contract that was illegal at the time of its formation. When one party did not know of the illegal performance of the contract by the other party, the innocent party can enforce it. In some cases, it is possible to divide the illegal part of a contract from the rest and enforce the provisions which are not affected by the illegality-this is called severance. The illegal parts of the contract can be severed if they are relatively unimportant to the contract and if the severance leaves the nature of the contract unaltered.

****

Ch. 7

Duress and Undue Influence

In this chapter we look at the effects that duress and undue influence have on the parties to a contract. We also look at inequality of bargaining power.

As we have seen, contracts are only binding if parties voluntarily consent to them. If one party is forced to sign under duress, the contract is invalid. As is usual, the law has developed two doctrines to deal with duress: the common law of duress and the equitable one of undue influence.

Duress

Although traditionally, common law has dealt with duress in terms of physical or psychological duress exerted when signing a contract, the doctrine has now been extended to economic duress. This, as the term implies, is where one party is forced into the contract due to economic pressure.

Economic duress first arose in *North Ocean Shipping Co v Hyundai Construction Co (The Atlantic Baron) (1979)* that concerned a contract for the building of a ship. As is commonly the case where duress is raised, the dispute concerned not the formation of the contract, but a supposed modification of its terms. Such a modification can only be binding if both parties consent to it. If one party's consent is achieved by duress the contract is void. Although the price of the ship had been fixed at the outset' while it was being built the sellers decided to raise the price by ten per cent, due to a drop in the exchange rate of the dollar. The buyers were not happy about this but were unwilling to risk delaying completion of the ship as they were already negotiating for it to be chartered by a major oil company. They therefore agreed to pay the increased price.

Eight months after the ship was delivered the buyers tried to sue the sellers claiming back the ten per cent because they said that it had been extracted from them under duress. The judge agreed that economic power constituted duress, the question being whether there had been 'compulsion of will'. This compulsion could stem from economic pressure as well as physical force. In this particular case the buyers were not allowed to recover the extra ten per cent. This was not because duress did not play a part as it did, but that they waited so long after delivery to sue, implying acceptance.

Economic duress will be present where there is compulsion of will to the extent that the party under threat has no practical alternative but to comply, and the pressure used is regarded by the law as illegitimate.

Threats of violence

In Barton v Armstrong (1976) the plaintiff threatened to kill the defendant if he did not sell his interest in the company they were both major shareholders in. The trial judge ruled that duress could not be pleaded since it was not established that the agreement would not have been entered into without the threats being made. The Privy Council, however, later ruled that a plea of duress should stand even if the death threat was not the only reason for entering into a contract.

Threats of unlawful restraint
In *Cummings v Ince* (1847), an elderly lady was told to sign over all her property or face not ever having a committal order to a mental asylum lifted. The contract was found to be void.

Threats to property
In *Skeate v Beale (1840),* the court decided that since the threat had been directed towards property, this did not constitute duress. However, in *The Siboen and the Sibotre* (1976), the court decided that serious threats that constituted burning a house or damaging expensive paintings should be considered as duress. Therefore, duress also covered property in the most serious circumstances.

Compulsion or coercion of the will
In *Pau v Lau Yiu Long (1980)* Lord Scarman listed the following indications of compulsion or coercion of the will:

- Did the party coerced have an alternative course open to him
- Did the party coerced protest
- Did the party coerced have independent advice?
- Did the party coerced take steps to avoid the contract?

Undue influence

Undue influence is an equitable doctrine, which applies where one party uses their influence over another to persuade them to make a contract. Where a court finds that a contract was made as a result of undue influence, it may set it aside, or modify its terms. In *Bank of Credit and Commerce International SA v Aboody (1990)* The court distinguished between two classes of undue influence: actual and presumed.

Class 1. Actual undue influence arises where the claimant can prove that they entered into the transaction as a result of undue influence from the other party. An example is where a person promises to either pay money or give goods in exchange for a promise not to report them for a criminal offence. The party claiming duress must prove that they were influenced (*Williams v Bayley (1886)*).

Class 2. Presumed undue influence will arise where there is a pre-existing relationship between the parties to a contract, as a result of which one places trust in another, and the contract between them is obviously disadvantageous to the one placing trust in another. Such a relationship of trust is called a fiduciary relationship and it may arise in two ways. It may fall into a category in which a relationship of trust is presumed to exist, such as parent and children *(Lancashire Loans Co v Black (1933))* patient-doctor, solicitor and client, trustees and beneficiaries *(Benningfield v Baxter (1886))* and spiritual leaders and followers *(Allcard v Skinner (1887))*. Where a relationship does not fall into obvious categories then a relationship of trust may well be established through, for example, effluxion of time or inherent trust such as an ongoing successful business relationship.

Where there has been a long relationship of trust and confidence between the parties, and the transaction is not readily explicable by the nature of the relationship, for example, between husband and wife or where one party had been accustomed to rely for advice and guidance on the other, the presumption in these cases of trust and confidence is irrebuttable. The presumption of undue influence where the transaction 'calls for explanation' is rebuttable. The stronger party can rebut the presumption of undue influence by showing that:

- full disclosure of all material facts was made
- the consideration was adequate
- the weaker party was in receipt of independent legal advice

One example of a fiduciary relationship is in the case of *Lloyds Bank v Bundy (1974)*. The plaintiff and his son both used the same bank. The son ran into business difficulties and the father was asked to guarantee the overdraft. He did this, putting up his farm as a guarantee and the bank tried to repossess the farm. The farmer claimed that the contract had been obtained by undue influence, on the basis that he had banked with Lloyds for a long time, and in that time had placed considerable trust in their advice, yet they had made no effort to warn him that it was not in their interest to give the guarantee. The Court of Appeal agreed that the presumption of undue influence had been raised. There was a relationship based on trust over time and the bank lost the case.

The transaction must be extremely disadvantageous (manifestly so) to give rise to a presumption of undue influence. This will be the case where it would have been 'obvious to any independent and reasonable persons who considered the transaction at that time with knowledge of all the relevant facts'. (*Bank of Credit and Commerce International SA v Aboody (1989)*).

Inequality of bargaining power

In Lloyds Bank v Bundy, as described above, Lord Denning suggested that economic duress was simply an example of a general principle of inequality of bargaining power. He argued that this principle allows English law to give relief to anyone who, without taking independent advice, makes a contract on unfair terms, or sells property for much less than it is worth because their own bargaining power is seriously compromised by ignorance, infirmity or need. Clearly, this is a key principle when negotiating and entering into contracts, more pertinent than simple undue influence as there is no suggestion that the other party had behaved improperly.

Illegitimate pressure

There must be some element of illegitimacy in the pressure exerted, for example, a threatened breach of contract. The illegitimacy will normally arise from the fact that what was threatened is unlawful. Economic duress is often pleaded together with lack of consideration in cases where a breach of consent is threatened by the promisor, unless he receives additional payment.

One case that illustrates this is *Atlas Express v Kafco (1989)* where Kafco, a small company which imported and distributed basketware, had a contract to supply Woolworths. They contracted with Atlas for the delivery of the basketware to Woolworths. The contract commenced, then Atlas discovered that they had underpriced the contract, and told Kafco that unless they paid a minimum sum for each consignment, they would cease to deliver. Kafco were heavily dependent on the Woolworth contract, and knew that a failure to deliver would lead both to the loss of the contract and an action for damages. At that time of year, they could not find an alternative carrier and agreed, under protest, to make the extra payments. Atlas sued for kafco's non-payment.

It was held that the agreement was invalid for economic duress, and also for lack of consideration.

Manifest disadvantage

In any claim of presumed undue influence, the agreement must be manifestly disadvantageous. In deciding whether an agreement is manifestly disadvantageous the courts will look at whether the disadvantages of the transaction outweigh the advantages.

Effect of undue influence on a third party

A bank may be deemed to have constructive knowledge of an impropriety if it has been placed 'on inquiry' that one of the parties has unduly influenced the other into entering into the contract. The leading case on undue influence is *Royal bank of Scotland v Etridge*

(2001). This appeal concerned eight cases of undue influence. In seven cases, the wife had permitted the family home, of which she had part ownership to be used as surety against her husband's personal or business debts. In all cases, the husband had defaulted and the bank had sought possession of the family home. The wife claimed that the bank had been placed on enquiry that the agreement had been elicited as a result of the husband's undue influence. It was held that three appeals were dismissed and five allowed. Moreover, the House of Lords provided important guidance for banks on how to avoid constructive knowledge of undue influence. The HOL also held that in that situation the third party could discharge his duty by making clear to the party concerned the full nature of the risk he or she is taking on.

****

Ch. 8

Third Party Rights

In this chapter we look at the rights of third parties to a contract. We also look at the notion of assignment.

A third party to any contract is a person who is not a party to the contract and has not provided consideration for the contract but has an interest in the performance. There has been a rule, long established in contract law, that only the parties to the contract could incur rights and obligations under it. This is known as 'privity of contract' this principle meaning that third parties could neither sue nor be sued under the contract.

There are two main aspects to the rule of privity. The first is that the third party cannot be made the subject of a burden imposed by the contract. The second is that a third party cannot enforce a benefit purported to be granted by the contract. This second rule has been heavily criticized, as it is inherently unjust and can lead to hardship and resulted in much debate and eventual reform leading to the Contracts (Rights of Third Parties) Act 1999. The privity rule has now only very limited effect. The Act has made changes in the way that contracts can be enforced by third parties.

The rights of third parties

The Contract (Rights of Third Parties) Act 1999 enables third parties to enforce contractual terms in certain situations. The Act applies to contracts made on or after 11th May 2000 or to contracts made during the six-month period after Royal Assent (11th November 1999) if the contract expressly states that the Act applies. Under the Act, third parties can sue in two situations:

- The contract expressly provides that they may do so; or
- The contract purports to confer a benefit on them, unless it is clear -that the term was not intended to be enforceable by the third party.

Express provision in the contract

Section 1 of the Act deals with this area. This enables the parties to expressly identify the third party in the contract.

The contract purports to confer a benefit on a third party

This is subject to an important provision that it will not apply if the contract expressly outlines this. The contract must specifically state that third parties will not benefit. In the absence of this then there may be a purported benefit to a third party inherent in the contract.

Under either of the above it is not necessary for the third party to be named. Nor need the person be in existence at the time of the contracts formation. The Act also provides that third parties are able to rely on a contracts exclusion or limitation clauses that are intended to cover them.

106

Consent to variations

The rights conferred under the Act would be of limited value if the contracting parties could at any time change their minds and remove the promised benefit. Section 2 of the act deals with the issue of amending and canceling contracts. The section states that unless the contract states otherwise, the parties to the contract may not rescind the contract, or vary it, so as to extinguish the third parties rights without their consent if the third party has either:

- Communicated to the promisor their assent to the relevant term;
- Relied on that term and the promisor knows of that reliance; or
- Relied on the term and the promisor can reasonably be expected to have foreseen that reliance.

If one of these three situations applies, then any variations or cancellations can only take place with the consent of the third party. Third parties to a contract have remedies that are available to them as if they were contracting parties.

Common law exceptions
Agency

The term 'agent' has a specific meaning in this context, and applies to an individual who makes a contract on behalf of someone else who is know as the principal. In the contractual sense, an agent is viewed by the law as an intermediary of the principal rather than a true party to the contract. In practice, one party to a contract made by an agent is usually a corporation of one kind or another, such as a PLC or a Local Authority, and the agent is their employee. There are three circumstances in which a party will be treated as an agent: where there is express authority; where there is implied authority; and where there is apparent authority. Express authority means that the agent has specifically asked the agent to make the contract in question. Implied authority arises where the agent is asked to do something where by implication a contract is to be made. Apparent authority is more problematic and arises where the principals past behavior gives the party to the contract reason to believe that the agent has authority to contract on the agent's behalf.

Assignment

It is possible to assign the benefit of the contract without the permission of the other party. A common example is where a small business with cash flow problems sells the debts owed to them to others who are factoring businesses.

Novation and assignment

A basic principle of contract law is that only the parties who have entered into the contract are bound by the contract. This is called 'privity of contract'. However, there are exceptions to the general rule, including the important concepts of Novation and Assignment

Novation

Novation effectively means to replace or to substitute. Novation in contract law is a mechanism whereby one party transfers all of their

108

obligations and benefits under a contract to a third party. The original party is extinguished and a new contract is created.

The obligations and benefits are the entirety of the contract in relation to one of the parties. For example, the clauses of the contract will include obligations that each party must adhere to, such as payment terms and giving notice within a set period. The benefits under the contract are what the party will received in return for its obligations (e.g. financial payments in return for supplying items).

In the case of novation, these contractual obligations and benefits will be transferred to a third party. That third party effectively replaces the original party as a party to the contract.

When a contract has been novated the other contracting party must be left in the exact same position as they were before the novation had taken place. Their rights and obligations under the contract will not be affected by the novation.

Consent to a novation

In order for a novation to occur, all parties to the original contract must agree to it – as well as the third party. The third party must provide some form of consideration (i.e. a price, such as money) for the contract to be effective. Consent to novation does not have to be given in writing. Consent can be given verbally, and it can also be inferred by conduct.

In practice, written consent would normally be given. In any event, the new contract following novation would effectively amount to written consent.

What happens to the original contract?

Following novation, the original contract will be extinguished and replaced by a new contract between one (or more) of the original parties and the third party.

Issue of consideration

Consideration (i.e. a price) is required to make a contract legally enforceable. There must, then, be consideration in the new contract. Alternatively, the parties can enter into a "deed of novation" removing the requirement for consideration to be provided. The discharge of the existing party's obligations and rights are, effectively, the 'consideration'.

When is novation typically used?

Novation is typically used in the following contexts:

- A design and build contractor in the construction industry transfers a construction contract to a new contractor;
- The seller of a business transfers the various contracts with his customers to the buyer of the business.

Collateral contracts

Where one party makes contracts with two others, the courts will sometimes use the device of 'finding' a collateral contract between the two others to evade the privity rule. An example of this is *Shanklin Pier Ltd v Detel Products Ltd (1951)*. The plaintiffs owned

Shanklin Pier, and needed it repainting. They contracted Detel to inquire about the qualities of its paint, and were told that it lasted between 7-10 years. The plaintiffs employed other contractors and told them to use Detel paint. The paint started to peel after three months and the Plaintiffs could not sue the contractors, as it was not they who had stated that the paint would last 7-10 years. The pier owners had no contract with Detel since the paint was bought by the contractors. However, the court held that there was in fact a collateral contract between the pier owners and Detel as Detel had told them that the paint would last, and the Pier owners request that the painters should use Detel paint was collateral for that promise.

****

Chapter 9

Discharge of a Contract

In this chapter we look at the ways that a contract is effectively discharged and also frustration of contract. We will also look at force majeur and the importance of force majeure clauses, particularly following the onset of COVID 19 and the impossibility of fulfilling contracts.

We look at the effects on the contract when it becomes impossible to fulfill because of the death of either party to a contract. Other areas are also explored.

A contract is said to be discharged when the rights and obligations in it come to an end. There are four ways in which a contract can come to an end: performance under the contract, i.e., natural end, end by mutual agreement, breach of contract and frustration. We should look at these areas in turn.

Performance under contract

This is the most obvious way of parties discharging their obligations and bringing the contract to a satisfactory end. In many cases, it is uncomplicated but there are some cases where one party may claim to have discharged their obligations and the other party disagrees. The law then has to look at the question of what constitutes performance. The obvious and general rule is that performance must exactly match the requirements laid down in the contract. This is known as entire performance. If the first party fails to perform then the other party need pay nothing at all, even if the shortfall actually causes no hardship. This is the simple rule and obviously contracts can be more complicated, with claim and counter claim. The case of *Cutter v Powell (1795)* demonstrates the difficulty. A sailor had contracted to serve on a ship traveling from Jamaica to Liverpool. He was to be paid 30 Guineas for the voyage, payable when the ship arrived in Liverpool. However, he died during the journey. His widow sued for wages up until he died, but her claim was unsuccessful, as the court held that the contract required entire performance.

Similarly, in *Bolton v Mahadeva (1972)* a central heating system gave out less heat than it should, and there were fumes in one room. It was held that the contractor could not claim   payment; although the boiler and pipes had been installed, they did not fulfill the primary purpose of heating the house.

The rule can also allow parties to escape from what has become an unprofitable contract to do so by taking advantage of the most minor departures from its terms. In *Re Moore and Co Ltd and Landaur and Co (1921)* the contract concerned the sale of canned fruit that were to be packed into cases of 30 tins. On delivery it was discovered that although the correct number of tins had been sent, almost half the cases contained only 24 tins in each. This made no difference to the market value of the goods, but the buyers pointed out that the sale was covered by the Sale of Goods Act, which stated that goods sold by description must correspond with that description. The delivery did not, and the buyers were within their rights to reject the whole consignment.

Mitigation of the entire performance rule

Substantial performance

This doctrine allows a party who has performed with only minor defects to claim the price of the work done, less any money the other party will have to spend to put the defects right.

Severable contracts

A contract is said to be severable where payment becomes due at various stages of performance, rather than in one lump sum when performance is complete. Most contracts of employment are examples of this. Also, major building contracts also operate in this way, allowing for stage payments. In a severable contract the money due at the end of each stage may be claimed and the person carrying out the work under the contract can refuse to continue if the payments are not made.

Prevention of performance by one party

Where one party performs one part of the agreed obligation, and is then prevented from completing the rest of the contract because of a fault of the other party, a quantum meruit can be claimed from the other party. Quantum meruit is an assessment of the amount performed to date and a reasonable price arrived at.

Breach of terms concerning time

The judgment here will be that of an assessment of whether 'time is of the essence' and the effect that completing the contract out of time has on the other party.

Force Majeure

The outbreak of coronavirus COVID-19 has caused, and continues to cause, great uncertainty for businesses around the world.

Force majeure clause

Force Majeure simply means circumstances beyond control A person or business will only be able to rely on a force majeure clause if one is included in the relevant contract and it applies to them. English law does not imply force majeure relief into contracts that are silent on the matter. It is very unusual to find force majeure clauses in English leases.

Simply because a force majeure clause exists (that operates in a persons or business favour), doesn't necessarily mean they have the right to invoke the relief in all situations. Force majeure clauses are typically drafted to include specified events (often called force majeure events). Whether the current situation constitutes a force majeure event is a matter for interpretation that requires specialist legal advice. It is unlikely that a clause envisages coronavirus COVID-19 specifically, however it may specify events such as pandemics, epidemics and work stoppages and also include events such as:

- compliance with a law or governmental order, rule, regulation or direction;

- any action taken by a government or public authority, including imposing embargo, export restriction or other restriction or prohibition;
- delays by suppliers or materials shortages;
- difficulty or increased costs in obtaining workers, goods or transport; or
- other circumstances affecting the supply of goods or services.
- It is also wise to consider how the outbreak is being classified by bodies such as the World Health Organisation at the time you're seeking to invoke the force majeure clause, as this may or may not support an argument or claim.

Force majeure clauses typically include a requirement, for the party seeking relief, to show that the event could not have been mitigated by preventative action. This demonstrates the point force majeure may only be invoked when the relevant event has prevented performance of the contract, not simply that the event exists, has caused economic hardship or that performance has become difficult or commercially undesirable.

Force majeure clauses typically include a requirement, for the party seeking relief, to show that the event could not have been mitigated by preventative action. This demonstrates the point force majeure may only be invoked when the relevant event has prevented performance of the contract, not simply that the event exists, has caused economic hardship or that performance has become difficult or commercially undesirable. Certain government agencies around the world have begun to issue "force majeure certificates" to some businesses in an attempt to prevent or stall breach of contract claims and limit liability.

Invoking a force majeure clause

The following non-exhaustive list contains some of the matters you should consider:

- force majeure clauses typically include a right for the unaffected party to terminate when the event has continued for a specified period of time. Although claiming force majeure relief may seem immediately beneficial to a business, it may have unintended consequences, such as triggering termination rights for customers;

- what do the contracts say? No force majeure clause is the same, therefore a one-size-fits-all approach will not work. Each relevant contract must be reviewed;

- have you communicated with your customers and suppliers? The outbreak continues to affect global trade and the number of cases and countries involved is increasing, so it may be that simple communication will suffice without the need to resort to legal action;

Force majeure clauses typically set out a procedure which must be followed to effectively claim relief under the clause. A person/business should obtain advice before invoking the clause to ensure that they have properly complied with that procedure.

118

Recent case law suggests that failure to comply can jeopardise subsequent legal claims.

Further considerations

When faced with such circumstances, it is advisable to have each affected contract reviewed in its entirety, as there are likely to be several terms that are impacted, including but not limited to exclusivity, liability and liquidated damages, delivery and termination rights, change control regimes, governing law and jurisdiction.

With Covid-19, there are countless ways in which one can imagine the impact of the pandemic on business and commerce. Judges themselves will have felt the impact on a personal level, and are likely to be sympathetic to anyone who seeks to rely on a force majeure clause. But parties should not assume that the clause will apply – the clause must be read carefully, and care must be taken to demonstrate that performance of the contract truly was rendered impossible or substantially more difficult as a result of the virus and its impact.

Frustration of contract

That an event has the effect of frustrating the contract is notoriously difficult to establish. Most recently, in *Canary Wharf (BP4) T1 Ltd v European Medicines Agency* [2019] EWHC 335 (Ch), the Court held that the supervening effect of Brexit did not render impossible the EMA's continued occupation of its London headquarters.

The basic principle underlying frustration of contract is that, after a contract is made, something happens, through no fault of the parties own, to make fulfillment of the contract impossible. Although there are many situations that can make it impossible to fulfill a contract only certain cases can be seen as genuine frustration. When a contract is discharged by frustration both parties are excused performance of their future obligations and the application of the Law Reform (Frustrated Contracts) Act 1943 determines what happens to advance payments (such as deposits and any other payments due) made before the frustrating event and claims for reimbursement for contractual expenses and performance conferred prior to frustration. Certainly, in the climate of COVID 19, frustration of contract is an obvious reality but it has to be proven in each of the situations highlighted below.

The modern doctrine of frustration arose from *Taylor v Caldwell (1863)*. The parties in the case had entered into an agreement concerning the use of Surrey Gardens and music hall for a series of concerts and day and night fetes. Six days before the planned date for the first concert, the building was burnt down, making it impossible for the concerts to go ahead. The party planning to put on the concerts was sued for breach of contract but the action failed, as fulfillment of the contract was impossible.

The concept and practice of frustration of contract can be placed in three categories: events that make performance or further performance impossible; events that make performance illegal; and those that make it pointless.

Impossible to fulfill contract

A contract may become impossible to perform because of destruction or unavailability of something essential for the contract to be performed.

Death of either party to the contract

Unavailability of party. Contracts which require personal performance will be frustrated if one party, for example, is ill or is imprisoned, providing that the non-availability of the party substantially effects performance

Method of performance impossible

Where a contract lays down a particular method of performance and this becomes impossible, the contract may be frustrated. A contract is unlikely to be frustrated simply because performance has become more expensive or more onerous than expected.

The leading modern case on frustration is *Davis Contractors Co Ltd v Fareham UDC (1956)*. Davis, a construction company contracted to build 78 houses for a local authority. The job was to take eight months, at a price of £94,000. In fact, labor shortages delayed the work, which ended up taking 22 months and cost the builders £22,000 more than they had planned for. The defendant was willing to pay the contract price in spite of the delay, but Davis sought to have the contract discharged on the grounds of frustration arguing that labor shortages made performance fundamentally different from that envisaged in the contract (it intended to seek payment on a quantum meruit basis to cover

121

costs). However, the House of Lords decided that the events that caused the delays were within the range of changes that could reasonably be expected to happen during the performance of a contract for building houses and the change of circumstances did not make performance radically different from what was expected. Therefore, the contract was not frustrated.

Lord Radcliffe explained:

'it is not hardship or inconvenience or material loss which itself calls the principle of frustration into play. There must be as well such a change in the significance of the obligation that the thing undertaken would, if performed, be different from that contracted for'.

Illegality

If, after a contract is formed, a change in the law makes its performance illegal, the contract will be frustrated.

Performance made pointless

A contract can be frustrated where a supervening event makes performance of a contract completely pointless, though still technically possible. A contract can be rendered pointless if there has been such a drastic change of circumstances as to dramatically alter the nature of the contract.

*

Time of frustrating event

In order to frustrate a contract, the event in question must occur after the contract is made.

Limits to the doctrine of frustration

The doctrine of frustration will not be applied on the grounds of inconvenience, increase in expense or loss of profit. The case above that highlights this is Davis Contractors Limited v Fareham UDC (1956). It will also not apply where there is express provision in the contract covering the intervening event or where the frustration is self-induced.

A contract will not be frustrated if the event making performance impossible was the voluntary action of one party. If the party concerned had a choice open to him, and chose to act as to make performance impossible, then frustration will be self induced and the court will refuse to treat the contract as discharged. One such case that highlights this is *The Superservant Two (1990)*. In this case one of the two barges owned by the defendants and used to transport oil rigs was sunk. They were therefore unable to fulfill their contract to transport an oil rig belonging to the plaintiff as their other barge (superservant one) was already allocated to other contracts. It was held that the contract was not frustrated. The defendants had another barge available, but chose not to allocate it to the contract with the plaintiffs.

Where the event was foreseeable

If, by reason of special knowledge, the event was foreseeable by one party, then he cannot claim frustration. This was highlighted in *Amalgamated Investment and Property Co v John Walker and Sons Ltd (1976)* where the possibility that a building could be listed was foreseen by the plaintiff who had enquired about the matter beforehand. A failure to obtain planning permission was also foreseeable and was a normal risk for property developers. The contract was therefore not frustrated.

Breach of contract

A contract is breached when one party performs defectively, or differently from the agreement or not at all (actual breach) or indicates in advance that they will not be performing as agreed (anticipatory breach). Where an anticipatory breach occurs, the other party can sue for breach straight away, it is not necessary to wait until performance falls due.

One case illustrating this is *Frost v Knight (1872)* where the defendant had promised to marry the plaintiff once his father had died. He later broke off the engagement before his father died, and when his ex fiancé sued him for breach of promise, he argued that she had no claim as the time for performance had not yet arrived. This argument was rejected and the plaintiff's case succeeded. Any effect of a breach of contract will entitle the innocent party to sue for damages but not every breach will entitle the wronged party to discharge the contract. If the contract is not discharged it will still need to be performed.

There are three main circumstances where the innocent party may wish to seek to discharge the contract:

Repudiation – this is where one party makes it clear that they no longer wish to be bound by the contract, either during its performance or before performance is due

Breach of a condition – Breach of a condition allows the innocent party to terminate the contract.

Serious breach of an innominate term- where the relevant term is classified as innominate, it will be the one that can be breached in both serious and trivial ways, and whether the innocent party is entitled to terminate or not will depend on how serious the results of the breach are. If the results are so serious as to undermine the foundations of the contract, the innocent party will have the right to terminate.

Even when one of these three types of breach occurs, the contract is not automatically discharged. The innocent party can usually choose whether or not to terminate. If the innocent party chooses to terminate this must be clearly communicated to the other party.

Agreement

In some cases, the parties to a contract will simply agree to terminate the contract, so that one or both parties are released from their obligations. A distinction is usually made between bilateral discharge where both parties will benefit from the ending by agreement and a unilateral discharge where one party benefits. In general an agreed discharge will be binding if it contains the same elements that make a contract binding when it is formed. Those that present the most problems are formality and consideration.

Consideration

Consideration is not usually a problem where both parties agree to alter their obligations since each is giving something in return for the change. Problems are most likely to occur when one parties obligations change. If the other party agrees to the change, their agreement will only be binding if put into the form of a deed, or supported by consideration. Where consideration is provided in return for one party's agreement to change this is called 'accord'. The provision of consideration is called 'satisfaction'. The arrangement is often termed accord and satisfaction.

Formalities

This issue arises in connection with certain types of contract (mainly concerning the sale of land) that must be evidenced in writing to be binding under the Law of Property Act (1925).

Remedies for breach of contract

There are a number of remedies available to the innocent party in the event of a breached contract. There are two main remedies, those under common law and equitable remedies. There is a third category that involves remedies arising from the party's own agreement. We will discuss remedies in more depth in the next chapter.

****

Ch. 10

Remedies for Breach of Contract

Finally, in this chapter we look at the various remedies available when a contract is breached. At the end of the chapter we will look at the effect of COVID 19 on consumer contracts specifically.

The principal remedy for breach of contract in English law is that of damages, which is compensation for loss suffered as a result of the breach. In the context of consumer contracts the Consumer Rights Act 2015 applies when statutory rights under a sale of goods, digital or services contract has not been met.

Damages

The usual remedy for breach of contracts is the award of damages to the innocent party. It aims to compensate for losses that result from not receiving performance that was due under the contract. In general the damages will cover both physical harm to the claimant and their property and also for any economic loss. There are very limited circumstances in which injury to feelings can be compensated for.

Damages can fall into the categories of unliquidated damages, which are damages assessed by the courts, the purpose of which is to compensate the victim for the loss he has suffered as a result of the breach and liquidated damages where the damages are set by the parties themselves.

General rule

When considering damages the general rule is that any damages that are awarded to innocent parties will place them in a position they would have been if the contract had been performed. There are, however, three limitations: causation, remoteness and mitigation.

Causation

A person will be liable only for losses caused by their own breach of contract. Acts intervening between the breach of contract and the loss incurred may break the chain of causation. One case illustrating this is *County Ltd v Girozentrale Securities (1996)* where the plaintiff's bank agreed to underwrite the issue of 26 million shares in a publicly quoted company. The defendants were stockbrokers who were engaged by the plaintiffs to approach potential investors in the shares. The brokers breached the terms of their contract and, in due course, the plaintiffs found themselves with 4.5 million shares on their hands which, the price of shares having fallen, represented a loss of nearly £7.5m. They sued the stockbrokers and the main issue in the case was whether the plaintiff's loss was caused by the defendant's breach of contract. In effect the plaintiffs would not have suffered their loss if there had not been a concurrence of a number of events of which the defendant's breach of contract was one. The Court of Appeal held that the broker's breach of contract remained the effective cause of the plaintiff's loss, the breach did not need to be the only cause. The defendants were liable for damages.

Remoteness

There are some losses that clearly result from the defendant's breach of contract, but are considered too remote from the breach for compensation to arise.

The rules concerning remoteness were originally laid down in *Hadley v Baxendale (1854)*. The case concerned a contract for delivery of an important piece of mill equipment, which had been sent away for repair. The equipment, an iron shaft, was not delivered until some days after the agreed date, which meant that the mill, which could not work without it, stood idle for the period whilst awaiting the part. The mill owners attempted to sue for this loss. The courts held that the defendant could not be liable for the loss in this case.

Mitigation

Claimants cannot simply sit back, do nothing, and let losses pile up and expect compensation for the whole loss if there was something that could have been done to mitigate the loss. It is up to defendants in this case to prove that the loss could have been mitigated. Claimants need only do what is reasonable to mitigate the loss.

*

Calculating any loss

Once it has been established that there is a loss and the defendant is liable the court must quantify the damages. In 1936, two American academics, Fuller and Perdue came up with two main ways of calculating compensation:

Loss of expectation (also called loss of bargain). This is the usual way in which contract damages are calculated and it aims to put claimants in the position that they would have been if the contract had not been performed.

Reliance loss. There are some cases of loss that are very difficult to quantify and in this case, the court may award damages calculated to compensate for any expenses or other loss incurred by the claimant when relying on the contract.

Action for an agreed sum (debt claim)

Where a contract specifies a price to be paid for performance, and the party due to pay fails to do so, the party who has performed can claim the price owing by means of an action for the agreed sum. Although the claim is for money this is not the same as a claim for damages. The claimant is not seeking compensation, but simply enforcement of the defendants promise to pay. One such case illustrating this is *White and Carter (Councils) Limited v McGregor (1962)* which was an action in debt therefore there was no duty on the innocent party to mitigate by seeking to minimize the loss covered. However, where the claimant has suffered additional loss beyond not receiving the agreed price, damages can be claimed alongside the agreed sum. An action such as this can only be brought once the duty to pay has arisen

Restitution

Where money has been paid under a contract or purported contract and performance has not been received in return, or has not been adequate, the payer may want to claim the money back, rather than claiming damages (if, for example, no additional loss has resulted from the failure to perform). In general this will only be possible if there has been a total failure of consideration so that restitution will prevent undue enrichment. This means that the party paying the money has not received any of what was paid for.

An action for money had and received where there has been a total failure of consideration (no contractual performance) is an example of a restitutionary claim. In this case it was the price paid for non-existent work to an oil tanker in *McRae v Commonwealth Disposals Commission (1951)*.

Equitable remedies

Where common law remedies are inadequate to compensate the claimant, there is a range of equitable remedies. However, these are not available as of right, merely because the defendant is in breach. They are provided at the discretion of the court, taking into account the behavior of both parties and the overall circumstances.

Specific performance

The common law will not force a specific party in breach to perform (except where performance is paying money only), even though this might be a fairly obvious solution to many contract problems. However, the equitable remedy of specific performance does compel a party in breach to perform. In practice, specific performance rarely applies as the making of such an order is subject to certain restrictions. Specific performance is only granted if damages alone would be an inadequate remedy. Specific performance is mainly applied to contracts to sell land since each piece of land is thought to be unique and impossible to replace. Where the damages are only nominal specific performance may be ordered to stop one party becoming unjustly enriched.

Because specific performance is a discretionary remedy the court will not apply it to cases where it could cause the claimant great hardship or unfairness. The courts will also allow the courts to refuse specific performance of a contract that has been obtained by unfair means. Some types of contract are unsuitable for specific performance, the two main types being contracts involving personal services (such as employment contracts) and contracts that involve continuous duties.

Key cases in respect of specific performance are *Beswick v Beswick (1968)* where a nephew had acquired his uncle's coal business and in exchange had promised his uncle that he would pay £5 a week annuity to the uncle's widow on the uncle's death. the nephew failed to pay and the court allowed specific performance, ordering the nephew to keep his promise. In *Co-operative Insurance Society Ltd v Argyll Stores (Holdings) Limited (1997)* the court allowed that a covenant in a lease of retail premises to keep open for trade during usual hours of business was not specifically enforceable because the courts would not make an order requiring a person to carry on a business. Any such order would require constant supervision and might cause injustice if keeping the business open caused a loss. *In Warren v Mendy (1989)* it was held that the court will not usually order specific performance of a contract involving personal services, such as a contract of employment.

Injunctions

Another remedy is that of the injunction. An injunction orders the defendant not to do a specific thing. Where the contract has already been breached the courts can make a mandatory injunction that will order the defendant to restore the situation to what it was before the breach.

Types of injunction

There are three main types of injunction, prohibitory injunction, which is an order commanding the defendant not to do something: mandatory injunction which orders the defendant to undo something he had agreed not to; interim injunction which is designed to regulate the position of the parties pending trial. Injunctions are also discretionary remedies and are subject to the similar constraints of orders of specific performance. However, an injunction will be granted to enforce a negative stipulation in a contract of employment, as long as this is not an indirect way of enforcing the contract.

Two cases highlighting this are:

Warner Brother Pictures Inc v Nelson (1937) where the actress Bette Davis was contracted to WB exclusively for a one year period, with an option to extend the period. During the period of contract she agreed to act for a competitor of WB. The court granted an injunction which prevented her from working for the competitor.

Page One Records v Britton (1968) where the 1960's pop group, The Troggs, were prevented indefinitely by their contract from appointing another person to work as their manager. The group were dissatisfied with their manager and appointed another. The courts refused to grant an injunction as it would prevent the group from working as musicians or would tie them to a personal contract against their wishes.

Remedies agreed by the parties (agreed damages)

Many contracts specify the kind of breach that will justify termination and the damages to be paid. There are two types of contractual clauses concerning damages: liquidated damages and penalty clauses. Liquidated damages is the term used where a contract specifies the amount of damages to be paid in the event of a breach, and this amount represents a genuine attempt to work out what the loss in the event of such a breach would be.

Penalty damages work in a different way. Some contracts, especially construction contracts, specify very high damages in the event of breach and they act as a deterrent, compelling the other party to perform. Where a court finds the damages laid down in contract act in this way, the relevant clause will be invalid and the party putting forward the clause must pursue damages in the usual way.

One case which illustrates this, and which provided for guidelines was that of *Dunlop Pneumatic Tyre Co Ltd v New Garage and Motor Co Ltd (1915)*. The plaintiffs supplied tyres to the defendants under a contract providing that the defendants would not resell them at less than the list price. If they breached this provision they would be liable to pay £5 for every tyre sold at less than the list price. The House of Lords held that the provision was not penal and was in the nature of liquidated damages. Undercutting the list price would have been damaging to the plaintiff's business. Lord Dunedin described the factors to be taken into account when deciding whether damages were penal or not, damages would be considered penal if the sum laid down was extravagantly greater than any loss that might conceivably result from the breach.

In *Makdessi v Cavendish Square Holdings BV (2013)* It was held that a penalty clause was unenforceable so that the claimant could recover his original loss.

Consumer contracts/remedies for breach and the Competition and Markets authority

There are a wide range of contracts that have been affected due to the Coronavirus (COVID-19) pandemic. The following sets out the CMA's general views on consumer contracts and about how the law operates in this area, to help consumers understand their rights and to help businesses treat their customers fairly.

The position in most cases

Where a contract is not performed as agreed, the CMA considers that consumer protection law will generally allow consumers to obtain a refund.

In particular, for most consumer contracts the CMA would expect a consumer to be offered a full refund where:

- a business has cancelled a contract without providing any of the promised goods or services;
- no service is provided by a business, for example because this is prevented by Government public health measures;
- a consumer cancels, or is prevented from receiving any services, because Government public health measures mean they are not allowed to use the services.

Limited exceptions to full refunds

Sometimes, a consumer will already have received some of the services they have paid for in advance. In those cases, the CMA considers that the consumer would normally be entitled to at least a refund for the services that are not provided. However, where they have already received something of value, consumers should generally be expected to pay for it and they will not usually be entitled to get all their money back.

In some cases, where Government public health measures prevent a business from providing a service or the consumer from receiving it, the business may be able to deduct a contribution to the costs it has already incurred in relation to the specific contract in question (where it cannot recover them elsewhere). In the CMA's view, these cases are likely to be relatively rare, however, and the costs that may be deducted from refunds will usually be limited.

Ongoing contracts

Where a consumer receives regular services in exchange for a regular payment as part of an ongoing contract, the CMA considers that consumer protection law:

- will normally require the consumer to be offered a refund for any services they have already paid for but that are not provided by the business or which the consumer is not allowed to use because of Government public health measures (this may be a partial refund of the total amount the consumer has paid, to reflect the value of the services already provided);

- will normally allow the consumer to withhold payment for services that are not provided by the business or which the consumer is not allowed to use because of Government public health measures;

- may allow a business to require payment of a small contribution to its costs until the provision of the service is resumed, but only where the contract terms set this out clearly and fairly.

Non-refundable payments and fees

In the CMA's view, the above rights to a refund will usually apply even where the consumer has paid what the business says is a non-refundable deposit or advance payment. The CMA also considers that businesses should not charge an admin fee (or equivalent) for processing refunds in the above circumstances.

Credits and re-booking

Consumers can normally be offered credits, vouchers, re-booking or re-scheduling as an alternative to a refund, but they should not be misled or pressured into doing so, and a refund should still be an option that is just as clearly and easily available. Any restrictions that apply to credits, vouchers, re-booking or re-scheduling, such as the period in which credits must be used or services re-booked, must also be fair and made clear to consumers.

Timing

The CMA accepts that, in the circumstances, it may take businesses longer than normal to process refunds. The timeframes for providing refunds should be made clear to consumers and refunds should still be given within a reasonable time (and, where there are statutory deadlines for payment – like those which apply to package holidays – businesses should take those into account).

Future contracts

Some contracts may require consumers to pay now for services they will receive in the future, after the current disruption has lifted. A business should not seek payments for a service it knows it will be unable to provide. Where the business reasonably expects to provide the service as agreed, the CMA's view is that, in general, the business can require consumers to carry on making these payments for the time being. That could be the case, for example, for some services due to be provided later in the year. Consumers' rights to refunds will depend on whether the services can be provided when the time comes.

Cancellation by consumers for other reasons

If a consumer cancels a contract because they no longer want the service, even though the service can still be provided as agreed, the consumer will be entitled to a refund in line with the applicable terms and conditions (on the assumption those terms are fair). The CMA has published guidance on unfair contract terms.

****

Glossary of terms

Acceptance (of an offer) - agreement to all the terms of a contract. Can be oral or in writing.

Accord and satisfaction – this occurs where one party's obligations under a contract change and consideration is provided in return for the other party's agreement to the change.

Actionable misrepresentation- this is a false statement of fact made by one party to the other which induces the other to enter into the contract, rendering the contract voidable.

Affirmation - affirmation occurs when a party, with full knowledge of its ability either to terminate a contract for repudiatory breach or to rescind for actionable misrepresentation, continues performance of the contract or acts in such a way that an unequivocal intention to continue performance of the contract can be construed.

Agent – a person authorized to act on behalf of another who is known to the main party to the contract.

Agreed damages clause - the parties may provide in their contract for the amount of damages paid upon breach.

Bilateral contract – where each party takes on an obligation, usually for promising the other something.

Breach of a contract – where one party does not perform, or performs differently from the agreement.

Common mistake - when both parties enter into a contract based on the same fundamental mistake relating to a contractual term.

Condition – a term in a contract that is an important term and a breach of this term would have significant consequences to one party.

Consideration – something that must be provided by each of the parties in order to make a binding contract.

Contract – a legally binding agreement, written or unwritten

Cross purpose mistake – where each party to the contract has a different view of the contractual situation.

Damages - damages are a financial remedy which aims to compensate the injured party.

Duress - duress is an equitable doctrine allowing a contract to be set aside because it was entered into under pressure or threat.

Economic duress – where one party is forced into a contract due to economic pressure.

Exemption clause - an exemption clause is a particular term which purports to exclude or limit the liability or the remedies which would otherwise be available to the injured party.

Exclusion clause – a clause that tries to exclude all responsibility for certain breaches of contract.

Freedom of contract – promotes the idea that parties should be allowed to bargain without interference from the courts.

Implied terms – terms which are not expressly used in a contract but which can be read into the contract.

Indemnity clause – provides that one party will reimburse the other in the event of any loss arising from the contract.

Innominate terms – these are terms that can be broken with either important or trivial consequences, depending on the nature of the breach.

Invitation to treat - an invitation to treat is an invitation to others to make offers as part of the negotiating process.

Limitation clause – this is where either party to the contract will seek to limit their liability for any loss.

Liquidated damages – this is where a contract specifies the amount of damages to be paid in the event of a breach.

Misrepresentation – where one party is induced to enter into a contract as a result of false statement of another.

Mitigation - the injured party has a 'duty' to minimise the losses it suffers following breach or misrepresentation.

Mutual mistake - a mutual mistake occurs when each party is fundamentally mistaken but each makes a different mistake, i.e. the parties are at cross purposes as to a term.

Novation - effectively means to replace or to substitute. Novation in contract law is a mechanism whereby one party transfers all of their obligations and benefits under a contract to a third party. The original party is extinguished and a new contract is created.

Offer – this is where communication is treated as an offer if it indicates the terms on which the offeror is prepared to make a contract and gives a clear indication that the offeror intends to be bound by the terms of the contract.

Privity of contract – this is where that only the parties to the contract incur rights and obligations under it.

Promissory estoppel - promissory estoppel is an equitable doctrine designed to prevent the promisor going back on his promise or representation that he would not insist on his strict legal rights under an existing contract where this would be inequitable because the promisee has relied on this promise or representation.

Quantum meruit – where a price has not been specified under a contract between parties but work has been done and a reasonable price can be claimed.

Remoteness - remoteness determines the scope of losses for which a party can be held responsible and so be liable to compensate the injured party in the event of breach of contract.

Representation - a representation is a statement which induces the contract but which does not involve any binding promise as to truth.

Repudiatory breach - every breach of contract will give rise to right to claim damages. However, unless the breach constitutes a repudiatory breach, the contract will remain in force.

Rescission - where a contract is voidable, for example for actionable misrepresentation, duress or undue influence, the remedy of rescission is available to the injured party.

Restitution - restitution allows for the recovery of money paid to the guilty party.

Severable contract – this is where a contract can be severed where payment becomes due at various stages of performance rather than in one lump sum.

Specific performance - this is an equitable remedy (and hence discretionary) which compels the party in breach to perform its obligations.

Subject to contract – parties do not intend to be bound by law until formal contracts are exchanged.

Terms of the contract – these describe the duties and obligations which each party has under the agreement.

Undue influence - this is an equitable doctrine allowing a contract to be set aside at the courts discretion.

Unilateral contracts – arises where only one party assumes an obligation

Void contract – this is where a contract is declared void, the effect being that there never was a contract in the first place.

Voidable contract – this is where an innocent party to the contract can chose to terminate it.

Warranty – this describes a contractual term that can be broken without highly important consequences. If a warranty is breached, the innocent party can sue for damages but cannot terminate the contract.

****

Index

www.straightforwardco.co.uk

All titles, listed below, in the Straightforward Guides Series, and further books in the Emerald Guides Series, can be purchased online by going to www.straightfowardco.co.uk A discount of 25% per title is offered with online purchases.

Law, Including Emerald Guides

Consumer Rights

Bankruptcy Insolvency and the Law

Employment Law

Private Tenants Rights

Family law

Small Claims in the County Court

Contract law

Intellectual Property and the law

Divorce and the law

Leaseholders Rights

The Process of Conveyancing

Knowing Your Rights and Using the Courts

Producing Your own Will

Housing Rights

The Bailiff the law and You

Probate and The Law

Company law

What to Expect When You Go to Court

Give me Your Money-Guide to Effective Debt Collection

Being a Litigant in Person
Conveyancing Residential property
A Practical Guide to Obtaining Probate
Marriage and Same Sex Partnerships
A Guide to Powers of Attorney
Mental Health and the Law

General titles, Including Emerald Guides

Letting Property for Profit
Buying, Selling and Renting property
Bookkeeping and Accounts for Small Business
Creative Writing
Freelance Writing
Writing Your own Life Story
Writing performance Poetry
Writing Romantic Fiction
Speech Writing
The Straightforward Business Plan
The Straightforward C.V.
Successful Public Speaking
Handling Bereavement
Individual and Personal Finance
The Crime Writers casebook
Being a Detective
A Comprehensive Guide to Arrest and Detention
A Comprehensive Guide to Burglary and Robbery

The Bailiff and You
Beating The Bully
Explaining Autism
Explaining Diabetes
Explaining Alzheimer's and Dementia
Explaining Asthma
Stop Smoking Now
Mind Power and Healthy Eating

Go to:

www.straightforwardco.co.uk